POPPY ROSE
SOLOMON

HOW TO
EDIT
YOUR OWN
NOVEL

First published by Poppy's Pages in 2025

www.poppyspagesediting.com

Written by Poppy Rose Solomon

Edited by Lizzie Augustine and Proofread by Rose Thomson

Cover design by Haylee Buswell (HB Pencil Designs)

Paperback ISBN: 978-0-6456986-7-1

eBook ISBN: 978-0-6456986-9-5

A catalogue record of this book is available from the National Library of Australia.

POPPY'S PAGES

The author acknowledges the First Nations peoples of the lands this book was written and published on. Respect and gratitude are extended to elders past and present.

Praise for How to Edit Your Own Novel

'A no-nonsense guide for writers ready to take their drafts from rough to refined. Packed with practical examples and actionable advice, *How to Edit Your Own Novel* will help you help you tighten your prose and revise with purpose.' *Tzeyi Koay,* author of *A Curse Carved in Ink*

*

'The perfect guide for writers at every level, delivered in a warm, accessible manner. It's like having a friend in your pocket. Poppy's wisdom and expertise is imparted in these pages. Every writer will find something useful.' *Bianca Breen,* author of *Made of Steam and Stardust*

*

'If you're dreaming of becoming an author, this book is indispensable. Poppy has included everything an aspiring (or experienced) writer needs to publish a well-structured, engaging and polished final product — including a comprehensive guide to planning, drafting, editing and publication, as well as exercises that are actually enjoyable. I only wish she'd published it sooner!' *Alice Woodland*, author of *Mooney River*

About the Author

Poppy Rose Solomon's creative pursuits are a manifestation of her passions for the whimsical and magical. Evoking inspiration and escapism is the goal of her storytelling. From her home in Lutruwita/Tasmania, she freelances as a YA editor and coach through her business Poppy's Pages. Woken Kingdom is her first series, with plenty more to come.

Contents

Introduction

I'd love to start by saying thank you for joining me on this journey. And, congratulations! Picking up this book means you're serious about being an author, and I'm really proud of you for taking this step. Writing and publishing books isn't easy, but it is so, so rewarding when we see creativity that comes from our hearts make its way out into the world. Our art helps people by giving them something to find comfort in – be it entertainment, inspiration, or empathy. It makes the world a better, bigger place. So of course we should encourage ourselves and others to make our creative dreams come true.

In this book, I want to inspire you, but I also won't sugar coat how difficult this journey can be. Those who know me know I talk – a lot – about how success in publishing is

99% in a writer's willingness to work hard. *Really hard.* And I'll repeat this over and over throughout this book. Writing and publishing takes time, and overnight success isn't common. Most authors making a living off writing are in it for the long haul, constantly putting out more work and improving their craft as well as their understanding of the market. They aren't making billions (or millions, or even thousands) off one book that happened to blow up and give them a lifetime of totally passive income.

This reality gets a lot of aspiring authors down, because they believe it should be easy. They feel entitled to their work being an instant bestseller without putting in all the effort it takes to create an amazing product (because if you want to sell it, that's what a book is). They don't want to research, learn, practise, and adapt. Many writers believe readers will love their work and they've produced the next big thing. Unfortunately, the market is saturated with incredible books, and readers are able to be picky. A book that doesn't grab readers, along with an author who doesn't market it, is most likely doomed to a life of invisibility.

But I know that isn't your fate, because by reading this book, you're showing you *are* willing and ready to work hard. You have the passion to become a brilliant author who can reach success. I'm already so excited for you, and I know you're going to produce some amazing stories.

Did you know that although most people would like to write a book someday, very few actually start? Fewer ever finish, fewer yet ever edit their work, and very, very few ever publish anything. Even writers with big ambitions often give up fast. You're in for a big adventure, but I hope it gives you some confidence that by being willing to learn and improve with your craft, you're already ahead of most aspiring writers.

Having published five of my own books (at the time of publishing this book in July 2025) and worked as a freelance editor on many novels – self published, traditionally published, and across many genres – I've been on both sides of professional editing many times and in many ways. I'm aware of more than just the *theory* of all the work that goes into editing or having your work edited. I understand all the *feelings* that come with this. The good, the bad, the monstrous. Sometimes as an author there are moments of pride and joy, and other times rejection, heartbreak, jealousy, and the temptation to give up. I'll say this, though: if you're passionate about stories, it's all worth it. Stay with me.

Publishing isn't an easy dream to pursue. You're met with gatekeeping, time constraints, the pressures of marketing, struggles to find your community, and the expectation to consistently be putting out more books. Yep . . . if you want a career as an author, you have to keep writing, maybe forever. But isn't writing the dream, anyway? If you choose to self publish, there's also going to be financial investments involved. Unfortunately, due to all of these hurdles, publishing books isn't accessible to many people.

Those of us who are scrappy and ridiculous enough to hustle and break through can still be met with failures, flops, and the greatest risk – never making a return on our investment. All this hard work, which is a full time job in itself, is usually done amidst the few spare moments authors get from their actual full time jobs, families, and other responsibilities. And you might never make a cent from it. It can be upsetting to go from an ambitious amateur writer to a downhearted published author who's realised the dream of bestseller status is pretty far out of reach.

All this to say, I'm nowhere near the big success we all dream of, but I'm still here. Why? Because I LOVE books, and my purpose keeps me going. Books help people to feel better, help us to learn, help us escape, and broaden our horizons. Writing books means contributing to millions of years of storytelling, a core part of humanity. That's what makes my heart full, so it wouldn't matter if I never made money off it, because I'm hardly going to stop. Some of the earliest artists, making cave paintings, definitely weren't in it for the money. Telling stories is the goal – capitalism and the need to make money are just an unfortunate piece of the puzzle. But if I keep going, I know that one day, maybe tomorrow, maybe in a decade or more, my writing will hit its audience and hopefully I'll be living off of it.

I believe every story is worth telling, and every story has a reader out there who needs to hear its message. Including *your* story.

My goal is to help writers like you break through the hurdles I've mentioned – and not just be empowered to jump over them, but bulldoze them right out of the way – so publishing can become more accessible.

To be clear, here are some things you *don't* need to become an author:

- A creative writing degree

- To pay a 'top' editor

- Expensive writing courses

- Wins from writing competitions

- Industry connections

All of these can help, of course. As I said earlier, publishing is a massively gatekept industry. I've seen this both as an author and as an editor, breaking into an industry that doesn't like to evolve. It'll be even harder for others, because I can only speak on my experience as a white Australian who has had the privilege to live with her family and create a publishing business without financial stress. Without that support, I wouldn't have been able to do all I've done.

Did you notice how I said I've created a 'publishing business'? Not to overwhelm you again, but I encourage you to remember that being an author isn't just about writing (and editing). There's marketing, networking, working with different people, and in general being a good businessperson. You're selling a product, so you aren't just a creative, but a business. The earlier you can switch into that business mindset, the better you'll be set up when it comes time to release your novel. Hop on social media and start building a presence as a writer, head to writing conferences and seminars, get to know your local booksellers – there are so many ways to get started.

While none of this is easy, it *can* be enjoyable, especially if you genuinely love books, storytelling, and creating a community of likeminded people. This is why I'm passionate about helping all writers gain the skills and confidence to publish their work. So many authors come to me with fears of everything they'll have to face – or I accidentally scare naïve writers after explaining all that being an author entails, so I hope that's not you as you read this book! – but there's a lot of good, too.

Being an author and sharing stories with the world is wonderful. It simply isn't as easy as it was five, ten, twenty, or more years ago when a published book would often sell itself. There's a huge amount of competition. This will only keep growing, especially with traditional publishers being pushed to pump out more and more books, often at a lesser quality because staff struggle with the workload, and the use of artificial intelligence (AI) to write books (something I'd like to note I am outspokenly against).

Are there any guarantees you'll be successful in this industry? No, although it depends on your idea of success. If you're serious about writing, you're in it for the long haul, and you're ready to put your all into it – mind, heart, and soul – you're in a great position to make something of this creative outlet you're so passionate about. Your work *can* shine amongst the rest. There's room for all of us. I want you to tell your story and I want to help you have the best chance of success.

By helping you improve and polish your work with the advice in this book, my aim is to empower you to present a shining manuscript when you get to the next step. This will either be querying agents/publishers, or going to a freelance editor to prepare for self publishing. (Many authors may even engage a professional editor before querying, because they know how hard it is to be picked up by an agent or publisher.)

That brings us to the two main purposes of this book:

1. **For the Self Publishing (or 'Indie') Route:** If

you're planning to self publish, use the advice in this book to make your manuscript the best it can be before engaging a professional editor. This will save you financial investment, because the editor won't need to spend so long working on your book. Plus, the more polished your manuscript is, the better advice your editor can give, because they can look deeper rather than be too distracted on more trivial edits.

2. **For the Traditional Publishing (or 'Trade' or 'Trad') Route:** If you want to be traditionally published, companies – whether it's a big 5 publishing house like Penguin Random House or Pan Macmillan, or an independent publisher, big or small – are looking for books they don't need to work too hard on. Their job is to find products to sell that will make them the most money, so they're looking for real gems. The harder they have to work on the book to make it a viable product for the market, the more it costs the company, because it takes the time of their editors (who are already overworked) and their resources. Occasionally they'll take on a book they LOVE the con-

cept of and will work with you to get it to a publishable state, but with all the time constraints in publishing, and the pressure on editors, this isn't usually the case. They'll only consider the best of the best – but sometimes being the best still isn't enough. They'll only take a chance on work they believe will make money (such as books with tropes they expect to do well over the next two years), unless perhaps you're already a big name in another industry and they're more willing to work with you to capitalise on your ready-made audience. Basically, no matter how good your book is, traditional publishing is incredibly competitive. You need a brilliant manuscript to get a chance, but even then, it often comes down to good timing and the right commissioning editor.

In self publishing, you invest in yourself. In traditional publishing, a company invests in you. Either way, because we're all businesspeople, a huge consideration in publishing is being able to spend the smallest amount of time and money possible to get the best return – a consideration that unfortunately often comes even before creativity and quality. (But let's leave that conversation for another time, because this is a book about editing, not a book about how much I loathe capitalism.) These financial facets are a major reason why publishing is so gatekept. Having money is a massive boost, as well as the privilege of being well connected, as these advantages allow writers to have more freedom and ability to a) write their book, b) polish their book, and c) be able to invest in getting it published and marketing it. Being a successful creative in our society can cost a lot.

Also, because publishers are cautious to invest in work outside what they believe will sell, they're often hard to convince to publish more diverse work. Traditional publishers usually look to buy books that meet genre expectations and appeal to a wide audience. More experimental work, work with high word counts (and therefore higher printing costs), or work that in any way is outside the publisher's current wishlist most likely won't be considered. On top of this, a huge majority of publishers and authors in the traditional space are white, and unfortunately, this means it's especially difficult to sell a novel to a big publisher if you're a person of colour with diverse characters. (Spoiler alert: diverse books sell to the market amazingly if they're given the same opportunities. Unfortunately, the dinosaurs of the industry don't want to hear this.)

Self publishing, though it comes with much more freedom, comes with its own host of hurdles. Publishing a book on your own means wearing a lot of hats, and not everyone has it in them to do it. Personally, after self publishing my first series, I'd love to get my next books traditionally published. Just to take some pressure off, if nothing more! As rewarding as being independent is, I find it difficult to do it all, especially with my ADHD and low energy levels. There's also the concern around marketing, because so many of us struggle to talk up our own work. But, especially in self publishing, we personally have to market relentlessly, and even spend our own money, for every single sale.

The decision of whether to go 'indie' or 'trad' comes down to a lot more than, 'I want pick my cover' versus 'I want to be in bookstores.' However, whichever direction you choose to take, there are always ways to chase your dream if you're willing to work for it. I believe in you, and I want you to believe in yourself too. If you're here, I know you believe your stories have merit, and you're ready to make the most of this industry despite the hardships that may arise.

And, how do we start preparing to give ourselves the best shot? Self editing!

In this book, I'll be using a funnel strategy to teach you about self editing. We'll start with the biggest picture aspects like characters and plot, and slowly make our way down to the smallest changes, like comma placement. My hope is that *How to Edit Your Own Novel* can sit next to you on your writing desk and that you'll carry it along on your journey through each round of edits (or drafts).

For each chapter, I've included an exercise to help you practise your craft and fully understand how to apply my advice to your unique writing style and project. You can read this book front to back, read it as you do rounds of edits and go through each chapter one at a time, or simply pick it up and read about topics you need some extra help with, when you need the help. Or, maybe you'll just enjoy picking up the book at random when you feel like doing some fun writing exercises! In any case, this book should help you become a stronger writer and self editor.

I'm so excited to help you create your masterpiece. Let's get into it!

Much love,

Poppy Rose Solomon x

1

Where Does Editing Fit in the Publishing Journey?

Before I start rambling, here's a quick rundown of what most writers' publishing journeys will look like:

1. The book idea arises.

2. Research, planning, and outlining.

3. The first draft – a rough idea of the story.

4. The second draft, or first round of self edits – a wide focus on developmental aspects.

5. Engaging a developmental editor (optional).

6. Third, fourth, fifth drafts, and so on as needed – narrowing focus on polishing prose, copy editing, checking for plot holes, etc.

7. Beta reads.

8. Another draft, with edits made based on feedback.

9. More drafts to polish.

10. The final draft, polished to the best you can get it to on your own.

11. Engaging an editor/querying agents and publishers.

Perhaps you've noticed that publishing a book isn't just about writing a quick draft that a publisher picks up and magics into an overnight bestseller. If you're in the early drafting stage of your novel, it could be years before you hold a physical, finished copy of it in your hands. Plus, several more years before you start to make any money, considering the time and financial investment.

Aspiring authors quickly discover that *writing* isn't just about writing. A lot of it is *rewriting*. And rewriting. And rewriting. Also known as drafting, or self editing rounds. The idea of editing many drafts might seem daunting, but it's the bulk of creating a manuscript. There's a lot more editing involved than there is getting the first draft down (at least, in most cases). You only *write* it once – then, if you're not doing full rewrites, you'll *edit* what you've crafted over and over. Draft after draft, with self edit after self edit, until it's ready for feedback.

If this sounds like something you absolutely don't want to do, or even refuse to do, then publishing a book might not be the path for you. Some people think they're above editing their work or having it edited. They may have huge egos and genuinely think their first draft is golden and untouchable. On the other hand, some people are incredibly sensitive to changing their work, because it comes from such a raw part of their psyche. Although this often stems from insecurity more than ego, this can be just as threatening to one's author career. If you can't edit your work or accept others' feedback, publishing isn't going to be very welcoming.

However, if it all sounds overwhelming but you're willing to push yourself through it, then publishing a book probably *is* the right path for you. The best writers are made from hard work and a willingness to learn, adapt, and take on feedback.

I'll give you a bit of hope. At the time of writing this chapter in October 2024, my sixth novel (fourth to be published), *Spellbound Empire,* is with my beta reader team, and I only completed two drafts before this stage. I've grown a lot as a writer, and my first drafts now tend to be strong. I also have the confidence in my work to send even these early drafts out. These days, I'm able to get a book out within four rounds of self editing at most, plus professional editing. In my case, this is mostly thanks to getting better at outlining and planning, creating a strong plot that I know will hit all the right story beats (similar to plot points, such as the 'inciting incident' or 'climax') and starting out with strong characters and worldbuilding rather than building on these aspects as I go. I can get into line edits more quickly, rather than focusing too deeply on developmental edits.

Let me clarify that the above method is what works best for *me*. All authors are different. Some take a lot of time and many, many drafts to put out a book, while others can produce work quite quickly. Some authors like to get each chapter perfect before moving on and may spend years on just one draft. Many authors outline and many don't. There's no right or wrong way. We all have our own process and method. When it comes to getting down the first draft, though, we can break up most writers into two categories:

- **Planners** (those who outline their books first before drafting) know exactly what they need to do and where to put each scene – that is, if they don't spend so long outlining that they never reach the drafting stage. Their first drafts are often cleaner and clearer because they were written with organised intention. However, sometimes outlining can box in the writer and make them struggle to pivot when the story calls for something different.

- **Pantsers** (those who write 'by the seat of their pants' with little or no outlining), may take longer to write because they spend a lot of time on discovery. They tell themselves the story on their first draft, learning as they go. This is a great way to get to know your characters and tell a story that feels very authentic. The downside, though, is that the first draft might come out with some beats in the wrong places, or the author may struggle to see them. The book can go on forever if they aren't careful to raise the tension and reach a climax. Because of this, they may also have to spend longer on developmental edits.

There are many kinds of writers in-between these two types. For example, although I outline, I'll have a lot of chapters in the outline where I know I need to get from A to B, but don't give myself instructions. These chapters are where I get to really play. On the other hand, there might be pantsers who, although they don't know the exact plot, go in having a really strong idea of their character's voice and development arc. The plot may not have to be airtight if the character arc is strong enough, because readers are still being taken on a clear journey.

Once you've written a few books and discovered the methods and timelines that work best for you, the process becomes much more streamlined. But when you're still learning, you will have to put more work in – just like with any skill you're developing. Rather than kick yourself in this phase while you learn, have some self compassion and let yourself mess up. Let yourself explore your creativity. Boxing yourself in or being unkind to yourself is the worst thing you can do here.

A caveat: Be cautious of writing too many drafts. Many authors are perfectionists and struggle with imposter syndrome. (If you're reading this book about editing your work to perfection, I think I can safely assume that's you. I know it's me!) We can fall into a trap of never feeling like our work is good enough, editing over and over. When you reach a point in editing where you're only making small changes in each draft, but you still can't seem to stop going over it to get it just right, it might be a sign you're overdoing it. Here, it's time to get it into the hands of a professional or get some beta feedback rather than continuously agonising.

Why is it important to self edit?

Are you wondering, 'But what's a professional editor for, if I have to edit my own work this much? Why are you telling me to do *your* job?' or even, 'Why can't I just send my first draft to an editor and pay them to fix it up, rather than me do all these drafts?'

Let's start with the purpose of the first draft. A piece of advice that works for many writers is to *write the first draft badly.* This early iteration of the novel only exists as a starting point. Rather than making slow progress by editing as you go, or worrying about getting it right, it helps to focus only on getting words down. Draft two is where you can start to make it good. The point is, at least by that point you'll have a foundation. You can't polish what you haven't written.

Even if you aren't trying to write a bad first draft, it's very rare that a first draft will be good enough to send directly to an editor. In this phase, you're still figuring out your characters, voice, and plot. You need to read through the manuscript again, make an outline if you haven't already, and start to identify what needs to be changed. This helps you go into the next draft with clarity on what to do next. With each iteration, you then keep rewriting until you feel confident that it's the best it can be in your hands.

By writing and rewriting, you're increasing the quality of your work every time (unless it gets to a point where you're being perfectionistic and never finishing), and this means *your editor will have much less to do.* Plus, they can focus on higher level suggestions that make your work great rather than simply fixing it to a readable level. If you send a first draft to an editor that needs to be entirely rewritten and lacks your unique voice and tone, the editor will have almost no choice but to rewrite it in their own voice. This is a huge risk of not self editing. It may no longer feel like your story, even if you created the foundation.

Why do you want your editor to have less to do?

Some professional editors charge a flat rate for all books, or a flat rate per word, which means that no matter what state your book is in, you'll pay them the same amount. I find this tends to be unfair to both the editor and client, so myself and many other editors charge based on how long we think it'll take to complete the edit.

We'll often offer a quote based on our hourly rate after completing a 1000 word sample edit. I calculate my quotes by looking at how long I spend editing 1000 words of someone's manuscript and how many thousands of words are in the book. I then multiply that by my hourly rate. *(*how many hours it took me to edit 1000 words* x *the manuscript's full word count divided by 1000* x *my hourly rate*)* Other editors have similar methods, such as giving their client a rate per word based on the same calculations.

A book that requires a more intensive edit is going to take the editor more time, so the editor will therefore charge more. Every manuscript that comes to me is vastly different, so it doesn't make sense to charge two authors the same fee. This is why, if you have a small budget, it makes a big difference to self edit the book to the best of your ability before the professional editor comes in. The less time they need to spend on it, the more money you save. Editing is an investment, and it should be one you consider wisely. Self publishing especially can cost a lot, so spending less on editing can mean you have more budget for a cover designer or for paid advertising. It's extremely important to budget effectively.

If you want to simply throw money at an expert to rewrite your first draft and turn it into a masterpiece, you're welcome to. I won't tell you where to spend your money. (Though you might be better off with a ghostwriter, in that case.) Typically, I turn away potential clients when their work isn't ready for me yet – I want us both to do our best work.

So, it's only once you've written several drafts, and you're quite happy with the work, that you're ready for professional feedback. Even then, it's always recommended to involve beta readers (who will often offer their thoughts for free). This helps you get a few opinions on how the story comes across to your target audience and helps guide you on your next rounds of edits before hiring a professional.

Are you crying and thinking about giving up, or are you ready to jump in? I know it sounds like a lot, and it is, but remember you're writing because it's a joy to tell stories. When it starts to feel like too much, that's when it's important to take a step back, relax, rejuvenate, and focus on things that make you feel inspired again – like going for a walk, having a nap, or reading other books. As long as you *don't give up*, you can achieve your dreams.

Exercise: My timeline

No matter where you are in your publishing journey, it can be helpful to write up a timeline, schedule, or a list of goals to help guide yourself on what you want to achieve – and clarify where you want to be, and when.

For some authors, this might mean working backwards, for example picking a date that you want to start querying or engage an editor. Let's say that date is March 2026, and today it's November 2024. To get through a few drafts, have a beta reading stage, and prepare for editing or querying without missing your deadline, you need to clarify what needs to get done and when. Your timeline might look like:

- **2024**

  - November, December: Draft One (Rough)

- **2025**

  - January-March: Draft Two (Focus on plot)

  - April-May: Draft Three (Focus on characters and tone)

- June-July: Draft Four (Focus on writing)

- August-September: Beta readers

- November-December: Collate beta feedback and make changes (Draft Five)

- **2026**

  - January-February: Draft Six

  - March: Final Pass

  - April: Start querying/send to professional editor

Of course, everyone's timeline is going to look totally different depending on their goals and how long it takes them to write and edit. For some authors, a draft can get done in a few weeks. For others, writing a book takes years. Some people find getting a first draft down really easy but find editing really difficult. The opposite is true for many others. Your schedule is most likely going to change as you go, but at least having one helps give you discipline and clarity.

The above example timeline also only includes getting the manuscript done. If you plan to query your book to agents and publishers, you'll have to add in additional tasks that need to be completed, such as crafting your pitch. If you want to self publish, tasks like getting the metadata, blurb and cover done are also important – plus booking in your editor and cover designer in advance. Either way, you'll want to start marketing early on, so this is an important step for your timeline. (For example, when is going to be the best time to focus more on building your social media platforms? Possibly when you're taking a break while the book is with betas.)

For this exercise, I want you to try creating a publishing timeline for your current manuscript, and see what it tells you. You can use the same layout as the example above, or create it in your own way. With your new timeline, have you found that it's going to take you longer than you thought to publish? Maybe you need to have some more patience with yourself. Or, have you given yourself too much time? Maybe it'd be a good idea to challenge yourself with a closer deadline.

Have fun planning!

2

Why Add Self Editing to the Process, and How Does an Editor Think?

Definitions:

- **Voice:** Your author voice is a blend of your style, tone, your characters' personalities, and the standards of the genre you're writing for. Great authors have strong voices that shine through in all their stories, like a thumb print that tells you it's theirs.

- **Beats:** Beats are the places in your book where plot points come up, such as the climax and resolution. For example, readers might expect the inciting incident at 10%, a midpoint plot twist at 50%, and the finale at 85%. Beats help the reader understand where they are in the story and help you guide the plot.

Poppy, you're scaring me! What's all this about time and money and effort? I just want to tell stories!

Hush! It's going to be okay. By getting into the right editing mindset, you can make this an enjoyable experience, I promise. There'll always be setbacks, and times you don't feel like it – who hasn't had writers block at some point? – but editing shouldn't feel like a chore. It's a huge aspect of being an author, so you should learn to do it in a way that's fun, that flows, and that works effectively for you.

It's time to get into the nitty gritty of the editing process. That is, what exactly is involved, and how do I want you to think to become a better self editor?

Getting into the editing mindset

Editing is a completely different skill to writing, to many people's amazement. Although many professional editors are also authors (like me), they're applying different abilities and knowledge bases to each job. Here's a bad metaphor: I have a brain that I use every day to do amazing things – but that does not make me qualified to be a brain surgeon. Honestly, I don't love to see authors suddenly offering editing services when they have no editorial training or experience. Having a few books published *does not* make someone an editor. Real editors know writing and editing for yourself is a very separate skill to editing for others.

In fact, most editor/authors will still have another professional editor edit their own books! I certainly do. Although I can self edit my work well, getting that second professional opinion (or even third, because I'll employ a proofreader too) is always vital. When we get too deep in writer mode, we struggle to catch our own errors or weaknesses.

But getting into an editing mindset is definitely possible as an author, or why would we be here right now? Yes

– getting an editor in the later stages of your novel is crucial. But for these early drafts, you're the one steering the boat. You need to employ your writing skills and blend them with your editing skills to maximise the efficacy of your drafts. (God that sounds corporate – *help*.)

How do editors think?

There are different types of editors, which I'll discuss more below, but all of them have a skilled eye for picking apart a novel (or an aspect of a novel), determining what's working and what isn't, and most importantly, suggesting how to make the novel stronger.

The role of an editor is complex, because they have to juggle two points of view and find the best way to get the best of both worlds. These are:

- **The author's perspective:**

  - What are they trying to do with the novel?

  - What do they want to get across?

  - Are they doing so effectively?

- **The readers' perspective:**

  - What do they want to get out of the novel?

  - Can they understand what's happening in the novel?

  - Will they be satisfied with how it pans out?

Finding this balance is the core of the mindset I get into as an editor. I'm not just there to 'fix errors', but to help you sell the book and help readers enjoy it. I want you to succeed as an author, so that means I can't simply stroke your ego and tell you you're amazing – though I'll always try to be positive, because I'm not there to crush your dreams! Instead, my job is to help you create a book that's going to be received well by readers and be positioned to make you money.

I have to be real with you when I believe part of the manuscript isn't working, or if I believe readers won't respond well. For example, if your characters don't feel relatable, if your voice doesn't seem like it'll resonate with your target audience, if the content is unnecessarily offensive or insensitive, or if you aren't hitting the expected beats for your genre and it could cause friction with readers. I'm going to tell you if your sentence structure is awkward, or if a word choice doesn't make sense.

However, I'm always going to keep your author voice and creativity as a top priority, because it's not my book or the readers' book – it's yours!

Utilising the editor mindset as an author

As an author, how do you replicate this mindset, blending different points of view to look at your novel at every level and see what the best direction to take is? The thing is, you can't be completely objective with your own work, and that's okay. If we could criticise our work from all angles and make it *absolutely perfect*, so it became a five-star read for everyone in the entire world, our books might lose their authenticity. It isn't possible and it wouldn't be good. We don't want one-hundred-per-cent textbook books, because they'd be robotic. Anyway, the idea of perfection is different to everyone.

When you go into your manuscript with an editing mind-set, remember that it isn't just about what readers might want. Just like the editor does, you have to find the best blend of what you want to do with the book, and what readers may be expecting. I'll say this a lot throughout this book, but *your story is your story*, and you should always keep that in mind before letting what others may think stamp down your creativity.

When getting into an editor mindset, ask yourself questions like:

- What am I trying to say with this book, scene, paragraph or line?

- Is the meaning clear to the reader?

- Does this plot point twist genre conventions enough to make the book engaging, without straying so much the reader will be upset their expectations weren't met?

- Are my characters' motivations always clear to the reader?

- Am I writing this book from the best point of view and tense to convey the story?

- What themes do I want to show through this novel? Can I make them more subtle, or should I make those themes clearer?

- Are the character arcs clear, showing strong development from the beginning to the end?

What training do editors have?

Are you wondering, 'Poppy, if editors are trained, can't I just get that training and be all sorted?' The reason I'm writing this book is so you *don't* have to go through all the training and experience, and can simply employ the skills you need to edit your own work. My editor training was expensive and a pain in the butt, as much as I'm glad I did it. If you want to be a professional editor (I'll talk a bit more about this at the end of the book), then go ahead and get your training. But for the purpose of this book, you are an author, and I want you to focus on authoring!

On the professional side, the ability to edit a book well, marrying the author's goals and the reader's needs, isn't a skill that manifests on its own. Learning to cultivate an author's voice takes lots of training and practise. An editor isn't just someone with a good eye for detail – though that's very much a requirement. They have an education in editing and fiction, and experience working in the genres they edit for. They should read consistently, staying up to date on trends and knowing what audiences are looking for, and be able to identify which books you're competing with. An editor's ability and willingness to continually evolve, improve, and learn is the best skill they can have.

Although many editors and publishing professionals will have a university degree in publishing, editing, English, literature, creative writing, or similar, this isn't necessary. More often, editors find themselves in the job because they've come from another industry and found that their skill for English and their attention to detail made them sought after by coworkers as an editor or proofreader. I've seen this across all sorts of industries, with even accountants, lawyers, and council workers turning into editors. When they realise their passion, they start looking into editing as a profession and seek out training and experience.

The older, more traditional route into becoming a fiction editor would be to:

1. Get an English degree (or similar with transfer-

able skills).

2. Take publishing internships.

3. Start as an editorial assistant or in other entry-level publishing role in a publishing house.

4. Climb the ladder towards becoming a senior editor.

This isn't easy, because publishing roles are so competitive and it's tough to get your foot in the door. Since most publishers are based in big, expensive cities but offer low pay, and don't have job openings often, a level of privilege is vital for many traditional publishing careers. But, times are changing. With the ability to work from home and freelance, more people (like me!) are building careers that aren't so traditional. You absolutely don't have to have a master's degree and years of in-house experience in a big 5 publishing house in New York to call yourself an editor.

For an author who wants to learn how to self edit, you absolutely don't need any of this complex experience. Anyone can learn the skills in their own way!

Maybe my story will help paint the picture. My experience started in university. I'd always wanted to be an author, but I chose to study journalism so I could write and keep improving my English skills while having a 'real' job. I'd never considering editing until my peers kept asking me to help fix up their assignments. They tapped into my skill before I did, and I quickly found that I *loved* it.

That's when I started to consider a pivot into publishing. I graduated and worked in marketing for a little while, but I didn't find it fulfilling, so I hustled to get into editing books. I took a gruelling and time-consuming editing course, marked harshly by experienced editors. At this point I had some experience, but this training helped fill in the gaps, taught me more about editing in other areas (I was used to fiction, and suddenly learning about tables and bibliographies – which I still despise), and explained what traditional publishers expect when working with freelance editors.

Do you, an author, need to have all this training, or spend all this time upskilling? If you want to, it can help. Having editorial knowledge is a benefit to authors, which is why I'm writing this book. But you don't need to spend a huge amount of money, or chase years of experience through competitive internships and low-paid work.

I do recommend being part of writing and editing associations to make use of the courses and workshops they offer. Memberships costs money, but they're worthwhile for what they give you access to. Plus, memberships are typically tax deductable if you're an author. The Institute of Professional Editors (IPEd) is the biggest Australian editing association, and the Australian Society of Authors (ASA) is popular for writers and authors. These associations help you improve as an author and self editor, and help you network. But, again, this isn't going to make or break your career.

In essence, what we're learning in *How to Edit Your Own Novel* is how to *think* like an editor, not *be* one. Although if you're thinking of becoming an editor, you can absolutely use this book as a starting point.

Here are some things I do regularly to try to keep myself up to date and continue to be a great editor, that you may or may not want to do:

- Completing industry research to look at what's trending, what's changing in how books are published, and what publishers are doing for marketing.

- Completing author research to find what authors need and create new offerings for clients, plus create resources like this book.

- Taking editing and writing courses, plus attending webinars, panels, and more.

- Attending writers' festivals, conferences, and author events such as book launches and signings.

- Listening to podcasts and reading books on editing and writing.

- Signing up to industry mailing lists and reading them to stay up to date on industry news.

- Finding ways to get work experience in aspects of publishing I'm less familiar with, like doing volunteer work for small publishing houses.

- Running social media accounts (including 'Book-Tok' and 'Bookstagram') to keep an eye on reader trends, and as a space to promote my clients' work.

- Reading and reviewing advanced copies of books to stay up to date on what publishers are acquiring and releasing.

- Reading widely in all genres to expand my knowledge.

- Working to expand my network, therefore expanding the network of my clients and helping to create opportunities for them.

- Keeping a database of trusted beta readers, ARC readers/reviewers, and sensitivity readers.

This sounds a little hectic even to me, seeing it written down! Remember this is just a guide of what an editor might do so you can better understand their mindset. You don't have to do any of the above, but it can always help you expand your skills and give your author career a boost. Networking, particularly, is very important.

What are the types of editors and stages, and how can you emulate them?

There's a lot of confusion around what an editor does. Often when I tell people I edit books for a living, they think I only fix typos. (Hint: I'm more than a personified autocorrect.) Or, if I tell someone I offer proofreading, they think that's the same thing as a copy edit. Many people believe book editors only exist in publishing houses. In short, first-time writers can find the full breadth of the editing profession very puzzling. That's okay – I don't know the ins and outs of rocket science, so I don't expect you to know the ins and outs of my industry. But that's what we're here to learn (editing, not rocket science!).

TL;DR: editing is so much more than most people imagine, as you may have begun to realise.

We typically split fiction editors into three categories (there's an even wider range of editors outside books, like academic editors, law editors, editors who work in big companies like advertising firms, and way more). You can engage different types of editors to help you at the different stages of writing your novel. Whether it's to have someone analyse the overall story and offer suggestions for improvement, or to have someone with an eagle eye do a final check before printing, editors have a range of skills, preferences, and offerings. For example, I don't like editing crime and horror, while other editors would hate to see books like mine – YA fantasy romances – in their inbox. I also tend to prefer copy editing jobs over developmental editing and proofreading, though I enjoy them all.

When self editing, you can get into the mindset of each editor type to ensure each round of self edits is holistic. Understanding that editing happens in stages will help you understand the 'editing funnel' I focus on in this book. Based on how edits are done professionally, in order from the widest perspective to the smallest details, each chapter in this book will focus on an editing skill you can implement in your work – and which order that step goes best in.

These are the three main types of editors, who are utilised in this order:

- **Developmental/Structural**
  - Advising on 'bigger picture' aspects and suggesting improvements.

- ◦ Plot and pacing

- ◦ Characters

- ◦ Worldbuilding

- ◦ Tone, voice, and style

- **Line, Copy, or Line-Copy-Blended**

  - ◦ Editing your prose to increase readability, ensure a strong voice, and correct errors. *(Note: Line and Copy are different editing types but often go together. We'll talk about this further below.)*

  - ◦ Sentence structure

  - ◦ Spelling and grammar

  - ◦ Word choice and strength

  - ◦ Tense, tone, flow, and clarity

- **Proofreading**

  - ◦ Checking the final, typeset file (PDF of the print book) with high attention to detail to fix errors before publication.

- ○ Typos

- ○ Inconsistencies

- ○ Formatting issues

At the top of the editing funnel is developmental editing, where we look at the work with a wide viewpoint and go over the major aspects of the story. Copy editing and line editing narrow into the writing itself. Finally, proofreading is right at the tip of the funnel, an eagle eye looking for last-minute lingering errors. Let's go into each editing type more deeply to understand better how you can utilise each of these stages in your self editing journey.

Developmental Editors

Developmental editing is also known as structural editing. Structural is easy to remember because if you were building a house, you'd put the structure up first. The land would be landscaped and a concrete slab would be put down, then builders would start putting up walls and the roof to make it a liveable house. So, these early-stage editors usually come in within the first few drafts of your book to help you improve it at a larger story level. This is bigger picture only and they won't be editing the prose itself except to comment on voice and tone.

You might be wondering if beta reading is similar, and it *can* be. While a beta reader looks at different aspects of the story and offers their opinion, they usually aren't a professional. They don't have the skills or training to give you higher-level insights and suggestions. A beta reader may answer your questions about what they like or dislike about the book, but it will only be their opinion. This is still often helpful, but it's a different kind of feedback.

A developmental editor will provide notes in-line throughout the manuscript, plus give you an in-depth report on the story. This can be many pages long, analysing all the overarching aspects of the novel, such as the tone, the plot, the characters, the character development, dynamics between the characters, the worldbuilding, adherence to genre conventions, and more. This is an expert on storytelling and an expert on your genre, so these notes won't simply be coming from the editor's likes and dislikes but from their professional, experienced, and more (but of course not entirely) objective perspective. They'll use their insights into each part of the story to give you advice on how to improve it, turning it into something that a) works well as a story, and b) will sell to readers. They may even work side-by-side with you, offering editing in a coaching style, in which they continue helping you across several drafts.

There are also manuscript assessments, which sit somewhere between beta reading and developmental editing. They're a bit like a mini developmental edit, where the editor still reads the full manuscript and offers comments that are from a professional point of view – just less in-depth. Rather than a 10+ page report on your novel, they may offer only a page or two with their major, most important insights. They may or may not leave comments in-line. Manuscript assessments often serve as an indicator of whether the book is sellable in the current publishing climate, if you want to first ask someone if they think the book is viable before you spend more time and money on it. Where might your novel stand against competition, what books are included in that competition, and how can the manuscript be improved to stand out?

Developmental editing is a huge job, taking a lot of time and skill. This type of editor usually has vast experience in writing and editing, and even publishing and marketing, because they need many skills to help you shape your novel and make it the best it can be. They also need to be empathetic and understanding. They're working with something very close to your heart, helping you build and improve *your* story, rather than simply turning it into something *they* think is good. A good developmental editor is effective at giving you feedback that uplifts you and improves the story from a professional perspective.

Developmental editing is usually the most costly edit. These experts may charge very high prices for their time and insights. For many authors, the value is clear, and they're happy to make that investment to improve their craft. However, you don't *need* to have a developmental editor. If you've already received positive beta reader feedback, or if you've already written a few books and can tell from your own self editing that it's overall sound in the bigger-picture aspects, you may not need a professional opinion at this stage (unlike copy edits and proofreads, which in my opinion are always necessary).

How can authors use developmental editing methods to self edit?

Let's think about the editing funnel again. I want you to consider why developmental editing comes before copy editing. Can you think of some good reasons? In the industry we always complete developmental editing first because there's no point copy editing each sentence in great detail when we're still changing overarching aspects. You may have to rewrite scenes completely, or even delete them. It's a huge waste to have painstakingly corrected every tiny typo just to not even keep what you wrote. That's why we have a funnelling system. It isn't just 'how it's usually done' – it's the best way to save you unnecessary time and effort.

I'm going to go into more detail about developmental edits in later chapters, where we'll focus in-depth on aspects like structure, realism, and characters, but let's look at some quick ideas of how to use a developmental eye on your novel:

- Create a timeline of events to ensure each plot point happens in an order that makes sense. Consider how many days pass between scenes – do you say it's Tuesday when it's actually Saturday?

- Create a character development arc for each main character, highlighting where they start and finish, as well as the setbacks along the way that force them to grow and change.

- Draw a map of your book's setting, whether it's a small town or a full fantasy world, identifying key areas and ensuring elements such as travel times make sense.

- Consider the tone of your book and if it's appropriate for the characters, story, genre, and target audience.

Copy and Line Editors

Copy and line editing can sometimes be confused, because the two editing types are similar and the definitions can blend. In fact, they blend so much that many editors just do both at once – like I do, because I find it most effective. Here are the definitions:

- **Line Editing**: Can sometimes come before a copy edit to improve the writing in terms of tone, voice, and style – the more creative aspects.

- **Copy Editing**: Focuses on spelling, grammar, sentence structure, punctuation – the more technical aspects.

- **Copy/Line Editing Blend**: The prose is looked at holistically by the editor, focusing on improving both the technical writing style and the overall feel of the writing.

It can be common in large traditional publishing houses to keep these two editors separate, and sometimes even use more than one copy editor to ensure the prose is absolutely sparkling by the time the book goes to print – and that it meets house style guidelines (we'll talk about 'style sheets' in the next chapter). However, this is becoming less and less common, as these jobs can usually be done by one person in one go, which is cheaper for the publisher. Similarly, it's much more economical for self publishing authors, because the more editors you employ, the more you're going to have to pay.

How can authors use copy and line editing techniques to self edit?

If you aren't familiar with Comments and Track Changes in Microsoft Word, I encourage you to start learning and understanding them now. It's also great to learn how to use Styles, as these can be very helpful when it comes to creating headings and navigating your manuscript. You can also use these features in Google Docs, but across publishing we usually use Word, because it's more secure and has more functions.

Many editors will ask that you send them your manuscript with specific formatting – and this is often the case for publishers and agents too when querying – so it's great to get on top of this early too. This includes the font, text size, headings, indents, and more. Here's the standard formatting you'll be asked to use:

- Times New Roman

- Pt 12

- Font black, pages white

- Double line spaced

- Aligned left or justified

- Single space after full stops/periods

- Indents of 1.27cm (0.5 inches) except the first paragraph in a chapter or section (note that this is standard for fiction; since this is a nonfiction book, I've used a different style here!)

- Headings styled as H1 or H2 for easier navigation

- Page numbers in header or footer

- Your name or pen name and the name of the book in the header (but be cautious of this for competitions, as sometimes they want entries to be anonymous and you might be disqualified)

If you don't get the formatting right before sending your work to a professional editor, they'll make these changes for you. This does mean that the time spent doing so could be added to your bill, so it's worth getting these things done yourself. Besides, they're pretty easy to do. I won't give you a full tutorial here, but go ahead and look online for instructions if you're confused on how to update your formatting.

On the other hand, if you're querying the novel for traditional publishing and sending the manuscript to a publisher or agent, you need to follow *very clearly* whatever their formatting guidelines are. Usually, they'll tell you on the submissions page of their website. Let me make this extremely clear: if you don't follow their guidelines, it's going to be an automatic rejection. They won't even look at your manuscript, because why would they want to work with someone who can't follow simple instructions? Agents and publishers have 'slush piles' filled with manuscript after manuscript from hopeful authors (so many that it takes them up to six months to give you a response, if they respond at all). They don't have time to look at the work of people who don't even meet their formatting instructions.

Although that's a bit of a tangent on formatting, it's great to get into the right mindset now and start doing things correctly so you're set up well for later. Even for self publishing, if you decide to format your book on your own, you'll want to get sorted early to make the process easier.

Hey, well done! Now your manuscript is set up for editing and you're familiar with Track Changes and Comments, you've already nailed the first big step! We're going to talk all about grammar, sentence structure, dialogue, tense, voice, and so very much more in the later chapters in this book, so for now I'm going to leave our notes on copy and line editing here.

Proofreaders

Maybe this is controversial to say, but proofreading isn't really editing, because a proofreader doesn't make suggestions on changes to the text. They aren't being creative, nor are they there to be kind or cruel. Simply, they look at the finished copy of a book – not just the final draft, but the actual formatted PDF version that will go to print – and make sure there aren't any lingering errors. They should be an objective third party (not yourself, not your editor, not your best friend who was good at English in high school) with an incredible eye for detail.

They check for any typos or inconsistencies in the writing, and also check that all the formatting looks right, including headings, page numbers, the contents page, and even graphs or images if the book has them (which makes non-fiction proofreading a bit harder!). This means they need a lot of the same skills as a copy editor or formatter, because they need to know what to look out for. But again, they don't actually *do* any editing or formatting. Like how copy and line editing are different skills to developmental editing – which are also both different to writing – proofreading is its own skill set. And a vital one, at that.

Allow me to tell you the most important thing about understanding proofreading, because this often confuses new authors, and often even editors who are new to proof-reading: **Proofreaders do not make any suggestions outside of correcting what's absolutely necessary.**

At this stage, with the novel formatted and ready to print, any changes can cause a ripple effect. Let's say the proofreader suggests adding a dialogue tag to a sentence on page 53. Maybe it's a little unclear who's speaking, and the proofreader thinks it would be better if a quick 'she said' was added. (Hint: better, but not necessary.) The author or editor goes back in and adds the dialogue tag, but this addition makes the paragraph go over another line. That edges some text onto page 54, creating a 'widow' (a lone word at the top of a page).

If the addition on page 53 means an extra page ends up being added down the line, then suddenly all the chapter headings will be one page forward. So if Chapter 16 is on page 245 in the contents page, which the proofreader has already checked, it's now going to be on page 246, introducing another error.

There are other problems that could arise, snowballing as more fixes are made to keep fixing things. Suddenly, it gets to a point where the book needs to be almost entirely reformatted and proofread again. This is worst-case scenario, but we're also only talking about one small suggestion here. If lots of unnecessary suggestions are given, we could have a huge problem. And since the proofread happens right before the release, major problems can mean having to push back the release date.

Unfortunately, many self published authors (and shifty publishers) who either don't understand the editing process or want to save money will hire a proofreader when they really need a copy editor. Because proofreading is the least intensive edit, it's usually the cheapest kind. So, people think, 'Well, the proofreader has to fix all the errors anyway, and they're cheaper, so I'll just hire them!' Well, I've been the proofreader on the receiving end of this before, and let me tell you, it's a nightmare. I'm a lot more careful taking on the 'wrong' jobs now, instead educating potential clients about what they really need. Again, having the book proofread at the wrong time can create big ripple effects that impact the whole book.

Like the other types of editing, it's always best to get a professional to do your proofreading, or at the very least someone you know who has a really strong grasp of English grammar and formatting, style guides, and an exceptional eye for detail. You can proofread it yourself too, of course, but (again, like the other editing types) a second opinion is essential. When you're too deep in your work, you start to miss all the little details, which means totally fresh eyes are best. That includes, ideally, not having your copy/line editor do the final check. You want someone completely different, as they're more likely to read each word and not accidentally skim or make assumptions since they're familiar with the material.

How can authors use proofreading techniques for self editing?

The main lesson here is to let your novel be done when it's done. Constantly making more 'fixes' and 'improvements' can keep introducing more errors, which puts you in a never-ending cycle. If we don't learn when to stop, we'll never publish our work.

Many of us authors are perfectionists, and since you're here, learning about editing your work, I'm willing to bet you're in that camp of people who would go over their manuscript over and over and *over* again to make sure it's beyond excellent without a single error. The thing is, as much as our perfectionism serves us in creating high quality work, it can really hold us back when it comes to trusting ourselves and our skill. We worry that a single typo on page 253 could ruin the entire reading experience and make us a laughing stock, with a mountain of one-star reviews. This blend of anxiety, self-doubt, distrust in others (yes, you need to trust your editor/proofreader and let them do their job), and imposter syndrome stops many people from ever putting their work out there, because they can't see it as ever being 'good enough'. Or, they think if they keep editing and proofreading it, maybe just *one last time*, it'll finally meet their impossibly high standards.

The good and bad news is that no novel is ever going to be absolutely perfect. Even bestselling novels from big 5 publishers will have some typos, even if they've been proofread by several people (we're all only human). For an 80,000 word book, say, a couple of typos compared to using the right spelling and punctuation tens of thousands of times is pretty good, right? Yes, it can be a little embarrassing when a reader points out a typo in your published book. But you know what? Being an author means having a thick skin, and constantly evolving and learning. You have to be sure enough of yourself that the little things don't get you down – otherwise, unfortunately, you may not last long in publishing. It's something we all learn as we go!

Letting go of perfectionism actually brings more creative freedom and makes you a better writer. Learning to trust yourself (and your team) opens you up to a world of possibilities, because you're not boxing yourself in due to fear of failure. You can be bold and confident, to the point that people barely notice a couple of tiny errors. I'm not saying don't worry about proofreading your work –

you definitely should! – but that having the confidence to make a few mistakes gives you far, far more benefits than the anxiety that comes with perfectionism.

How do editors present their feedback? (Being kind – to yourself!)

Handing your work over to an editor can be scary. Honestly, it kind of *always* is. Even for me, with four books edited by editors I trust deeply, giving my work to someone and asking them to tell me exactly what's wrong with it is pretty uncomfortable.

However, an editor's job isn't to hurt your feelings, bully you, put you down, or make you feel small. Their job is to help you improve and make you feel excited about how you can take your beautiful work and make it even better. This is why I love being an editor. It's such a huge privilege to be allowed access into something so deep to someone's heart and help them turn it into something they can share with the world. A good editor, whether developmental or copy/line, will hold your hand and encourage you, while also being honest about what isn't working in your manuscript – while guiding you towards how to make it work. What's the lesson here? **Being kind to yourself!**

Let's say there's a sentence in a manuscript like:

Thea gave Randal the remote control, very irritated, and yells at him to just pick his own show if he was going to keep talking.

The two big drawbacks here are that the tense changes halfway through then goes back, and it's written in *tell* rather than *show*. Here are two options for how I could comment on this and suggest a rewrite:

a) Why does the tense change and then go back? You should know how to write tense properly. It's also telling instead of showing, so I think you should rewrite it to be better like this . . .

b) While this line is clear on Thea's frustration, it could be improved by, for example, changing 'gave' to 'tossed' to show that anger. The frustration is also showed when she yells at him, so we can cut the 'very irritated' to avoid overwriting. Also, be cautious of changing tense – it's important to stick to just past or present. Here's an example of what I mean to improve this line . . .

One of these is a lot easier to take than the other, right? While option A is quite rude and unempathetic, especially to someone who's probably early in their writing journey if they're struggling this much with tense, option B offers understanding of what they're trying to say and gentle suggestions. Not only that, but option B actually explains *why* the editor has made the suggestions, which goes a long way. They aren't admonishing the writer for making mistakes, but guiding them towards getting it right.

Here's my rewrite of the line, though I might not change it quite this much in a real scenario, as I'd want to respect the author's voice:

Thea threw Randal the remote control. 'Just pick your own show if you're gonna keep talking!'

When we identify errors or weaknesses in our own writing, it's easy to put ourselves down. 'Why would I write *that*?' 'I already know this rule, how did I forget to X?' 'Who puts a comma like that!' 'No one talks like that in real life.' 'I'll never be good at this. I should just quit!'

But what does talking to yourself like this accomplish? It only makes you feel bad. It discourages you from continuing and learning from your mistakes, which is how you grow and become a good author. As I've mentioned before, your early drafts, especially the first one, are going to be riddled with weaknesses and errors. That's because draft one is only for you to get an understanding of the story – it's not about getting the actual storytelling perfect. If you judge yourself based on your early drafts, you're only going to lower your self-esteem and push yourself back from success. Even in later drafts, there are going to be errors, and as you improve with each draft, there'll be new ideas you'll want to implement to make your writing stronger.

Thank your past self for laying the foundations for you, and be proud of your current self for all you've learned.

When you're kind to yourself in edits, just like the example above of the kind editor versus the rude editor, you build yourself up. You see how much you improve and learn with each rewrite, and you get to feel pride in yourself. You get to be confident, and you should be, because you're creating something great and putting your ego aside to make it worth sharing.

How do you know when to accept criticism?

We should also talk about being able to accept criticism and feedback. Whether suggestions are coming from a professional, from a friend or family member, or from yourself, there's a point where you have to make the decision to either accept what was said and make a change, or decline it and stand your ground.

This is a huge grey area. I'm never going to tell you to accept every single piece of feedback, and I'm also never going to tell you to ignore everything others say and just do what you want. If you strongly disagree with, say, a piece of writing advice you heard online, you don't have to follow it just because someone said you should. There are so many people on the internet saying all kinds of incorrect things, or things may be kind-of correct but don't apply to your story. Similarly, if you strongly disagree with a beta reader's note on your story (for example, they say something you wrote was unclear and that you should change it, but you made it unclear on purpose) you're also very welcome to ignore their thoughts. If something in your story is really important to you and your gut feeling is to keep it the way it is, be cautious of allowing one person's feedback to shatter your self confidence – it's your book, after all.

However, if you have several people giving you the same feedback, e.g. they all think the book would flow better in first person instead of third, then you might have to put your ego aside and really consider taking the note. Criticism can hurt, and it's the place where we writers have to make our toughest decisions and really think about if our resistance to changing something in the book is coming from our gut feeling about how the book needs to be told, or our hurt feelings.

In the end: stay strong, be kind to yourself, and remember it's *your* story, not anyone else's.

Exercise: Edit your book

There are two main ways editors will mark up your manuscript – Track Changes and Comments (yes, like we discussed under copy and line editing!). Open a new Word or Google Docs document and paste in a passage of your book (300-1000 words, depending on how energised you feel). Make sure Track Changes (in Word) or editing mode (Docs) is turned on. Have a play with Track Changes and adding Comments to learn how to use both if you haven't already.

Now, read through the passage as objectively as possible, thinking as a reader would when you move through each line. Use Track Changes to fix typos (but don't accept the changes – I want you to see them all at the end) and add Comments to make suggestions such as where dialogue could be improved or to note where things don't quite make sense – and remember, word your notes kindly!

Put it aside for a few days then go back to see your edits again. Is there anything you'd change now, with fresh eyes? Were your comments useful, kind, and helpful?

3

Style Sheets - You're in Charge

When I was in school, I actually struggled with English class. I'm not someone who has a knack for this stuff naturally – my ADHD didn't want me to learn about all of that at all. My teachers drilled into me, over and over, all these rules that did my head in. I got decent grades in the end, due to a silly amount of hard work. But I just wanted to write and enjoy it! I wanted to show off my creativity in ways that teachers only wanted to stifle. The thing is, so much of what we learn in school, so many of the rules we're punished for not following, are meant to be bent and broken in the real world.

This might sound mad coming from me, but grammar rules *aren't* always the right way to go in creative writing. This is because fiction – particularly your character's voice – isn't always going to be correct! (Sorry if that knocks any perfectionists off their high horses or breaks any hearts.) One of the first things they taught me when I started studying communications at university was to throw away most of what I was taught in high school English. Out here in the real world, there's a lot more flexibility when it comes to the rules. In school we're taught to follow, but if we want to be creatives, or good at our jobs, we have to learn to break out of boxes and do our own thing. Bending rules is, kind of, the core of creativity.

So much of the English language is subjective. Most companies – across all industries, but especially publishing houses – have their own style guides, because there are so many ways to write things (do we use en dashes or em dashes, for example). Let's say you're Australian but use some Americanised spelling, because the majority of your audience is from the US. Is that wrong? Not necessarily! No matter who says what, ultimately your style is your choice. You can write your entire book in Comic Sans if you really want to.

So, what's most important? *Consistency.*

As an editor, I don't care if you use single or double quote marks for your dialogue. What I do care about is that you use the same throughout, so the reader doesn't get confused. Consistency gives you authority and keeps the writing invisible – and this is one of the ways we get readers to fully engage in and fall into our stories. If there are inconsistencies, like using *colour* sometimes and *color* other times, the reader starts to notice, even subconsciously. We notice patterns as humans, and when something strays, it jars us. This is why, although I don't care which spelling you use (though *colour* is better, obviously!) I need you to pick the rules you're going to stick to, and stick to them.

Just like we touched on in the last chapter, in regards to not allowing editors or readers to trample your unique voice, this chapter is all about you being the boss. Wherever you are right now, stretch your back up straight and take a second to sit in your authority. I hereby crown *you* the queen, king, or ungendered leader of your novel. Congratulations, your majesty! You'll make the style decisions (unless your publisher has their own style guide they want you to use, but that's way down the line), which means it's all in your hands.

This is both a positive and negative, depending on how you look at it. On one hand, you get to choose your own style. On the other, this leaves you with some responsibility. It might feel overwhelming, new, and uncomfortable. So, why is it important to get on top of your style now and not leave it for your editor, agent, or publisher?

- **Editors**: Editors look for consistency. If you don't provide them with a style sheet, they'll usually make one based on which conventions you use most. Having to go through your manuscript and update every instance of inconsistency *and* create the style sheet adds time, therefore potentially adding to their fee.

- **Agents/Publishers**: They're looking for authors who not only have a great grasp of English, but who have a strong voice, and understand concepts like consistent style. If you don't show this through your work, they may not take you as seriously. If it comes down to your book or someone else's who has stronger style and therefore seems easier to work with, you might end up being rejected.

How about a real life example of breaking rules well by doing it consistently? Sally Roony, author of bestselling and beloved books like *Normal People* (2018) and *Conversations With Friends* (2017), has faced backlash for not using quote marks in her books. Many readers find it almost unbearable to read, or simply don't give her books a chance since they sit outside the conventions they're so used to. They utterly reject the idea of her books without giving them a try, or even find themselves angry that she'd dare to break such an 'important rule' in the first place.

This is up to interpretation, and I'm not saying you should feel one way or the other about it. Personally, I enjoy the way Rooney breaks the rules by not using quote marks, and find that her books are a fantastic example of using unique style conventions while still creating a very effective novel. Though it takes a bit of getting used to, the way her prose is written makes it quite clear when someone is speaking, and who is speaking. In fact, the lack of quote marks and therefore less punctuation makes the writing flow very well. The use of too much punctuation can get us stuck as readers, as it can stand out (as it should, because it's a signal to the reader), so writing with less of it creates a highly engaging effect.

Let me be clear: I'm not saying you should go and write a book without quote marks. I'm not convinced most people could, at least not to the level that Rooney does, because her writing is strong enough to speak for itself without needing them. This is what I mean about breaking the rules well – it isn't just about doing your own thing, but doing your own thing *strategically* and *successfully*. Every author will have fans and haters, but you want the majority of your readers to at least understand what you're going for. Don't make unconventional style choices just for shock factor or to show off. They should always add to the story.

How do editors see style?

From an editor's perspective, I'm not just an expert in English, but an expert in knowing my clients' genres and target audiences. This is why I like to work primarily with YA and fantasy – it's what I read and write the most, so I'm most confident here in helping you improve it and sell it. Plus, I'm an expert in cultivating your voice to show your unique craft, show your character's personalities, and also meet the conventions your audience expects. (This isn't me pitching myself, but damn I sound great right now . . .)

Editing isn't about 'perfect' English – it's about ensuring the author's voice comes across in the most effective way. Understanding your voice, characters, themes, and intentions means that an editor needs many more skills than just knowing English rules. They need to know how to *break* the rules. This is also really important for you to understand when it comes to creating your personal style.

How often do you speak out loud in grammatically correct sentences? I dare you to record yourself talking for a minute then see if it's even possible to write it down in a coherent way. Most of us have our very own language and form of communication, completely unique to us, despite existing in the broader category of 'English speaker'. I grew up by the beach in Australia, surrounded by 'bogans' who talked loudly, casually, and with strong Queensland accents. Compare that to someone who grew up in the city, went to posh schools, and is now CEO of a major company . . . they probably have a totally different grasp of language. Even if not everyone gets it, because not all writing styles mesh with all readers, it's ultimately up to you to write in a way that feels authentic to yourself and your characters.

Here are some ways writers differ:

- Past tense *or* present tense

- First, second *or* third person

- UK *or* US spelling

- Lots of description *or* less description

- Flowery, poetic writing *or* simple and concise writing

- Lots of niche slang *or* more generic language

- Formal *or* conversational tone

We'll discuss lots of these points later in this book, but for now, the thing to understand is that you're in charge and you should make decisions based on what's best for you and your story – not what anyone else thinks.

What are style sheets?

I love a good style sheet (or style guide). When I receive a manuscript for an edit and it has one already, I know this author means business. Why? Because they already have all their grammar and spelling decisions made and laid out easy-to-find, making my job much easier. If I receive a book from a client and it doesn't have a style sheet, I'll make one. It's an important resource for any editor, author, proofreader, or formatter – really, it's vital for everyone involved in the making of a book – so I'll make sure every book I work on gets one.

What is it? It's all in the name. A style sheet is . . . a sheet about style. For fiction books, it lays out all the stylistic choices unique to the manuscript, as well as the characters and place names – even descriptions of people, places, and other important aspects to ensure consistency. There may be a timeline included, which is an amazing tool for avoiding plot holes. And if the book has complex worldbuilding, such as a magic system, or many places, countries, families, history, religions, etc. the guide can include these so nothing ever gets forgotten or lost along the way.

It's also the nitty gritty aspects like whether you use en dashes or em dashes, and where. If you like Oxford commas or not, or if you use UK or US spelling or even a blend of both. Are you sitting there going, 'Why on earth is all that even important? Who cares what dash I use where?' Just to drill it in further, consistency makes a book professional and makes the writing more invisible to readers – it means that instead of being caught up on typos and inconsistencies, they can get lost in the story.

If your writing is inconsistent, it decreases your authority in the eyes of the reader. Trust is lost, and so is engagement.

That said, sometimes consistency can be broken. For example, I typically use an Oxford comma (which is adding a comma before 'and' in a list, e.g. *red, blue, and green*), but in action scenes I'll often take them out to speed up how quickly the reader is reading – rather than slowing them down with extra punctuation.

In some cases, when you're writing from more than one point of view in a story, you can change the styling to make each character feel different. You might even introduce some typos on purpose, for example if you're writing a diary entry from the perspective of a child – as this would make it feel more realistic.

Right now, I'm guessing you're either super excited about all the ways you can play with writing style, or you're overwhelmed and baffled. If you're confused, that would make a lot of sense. Why am I teaching you about the importance of rules and consistency just to then tell you to do whatever? Make it make sense, Poppy!

In fiction, there truly aren't any rules that can't be broken. We follow them as much as possible – these pieces of advice are there for a reason, because they tend to work – but ultimately, we're in charge of our own narrative. Just like in real life, not to get too philosophical. The rules are our foundation, our building blocks, and they keep us in line. But deviating can create awesome impact.

The thing about good writing and good editing is that we can accept both truths – that consistency is vital *and* telling the story in the best way possible is vital. This is a big key to creating a well-written book. Perfection is a book with writing that usually remains 'invisible' so readers can get lost in the story, but occasionally breaks

the rules with such creativity and intention that it really
packs a punch.

What's in a style sheet?

Now you believe me about how important style is, let's
go over your style sheet step-by-step. I've put the *actual
style sheet used for this book* in the 'Resources' section
at the end, so you can see a real-life example. Usually
the layout of a style sheet will be in two columns, but
there's no right or wrong way to do it as long as it's clear,
functional, and includes everything necessary for your
book. Alphabetical order also goes a long way, as it makes
things easier to find.

Punctuation

- Single or double quote marks

- Ellipses spaced or together, and against words
  either side or spaced (. . . versus ...)

- En dash and em dash use

- Compound words hyphenated or not hyphenated
  – if not hyphenated, open or closed, e.g. *note book*
  versus *notebook* (If any words are outside your
  usual hyphenation rules, add them into the **A-Z**
  with how you want them formatted)

- Oxford comma or no

A-Z of spelling

- UK or US English

- Columns with an entry for each letter so the
  author, editor or proofreader can easily check
  spellings (like a dictionary) – this doesn't mean
  every word used in the book, but any words with
  different options such as *analysed* and *analyzed*

- Any spellings you often confuse so you and your
  editor know to double check them (I struggle with
  affect and *effect*!)

- Words with inflections, such as naïve

- Different spellings that are correct but have

changed in popularity over time, such as *alright* versus *all right*

Capitalisation

- Words that are capitalised that might not usually be, outside of specific context, for example *the Princess* instead of *the princess*, *sir* or *Sir,* or words you've made up or words that are specific to the world of the novel, for example capitalising *Magic* or a job/hobby in the world like *Potion Maker.*

- Heading style sentence case or title case

- Small caps usage

- If using all-caps for emphasis is allowed, e.g. a character shouting, STOP IT!

Special formatting

- Bold or italics usage for emphasis

- How thoughts are formatted, e.g. in italics to show direct inner monologue

- Italics for words in other languages

- Italics for names of other works like movies or brands

- Italics for quotes

- Italics for cursing, or made-up swears

Flashbacks/Alternate Points of View

- Italics or other formatting

- Change of tense

- Change in dialogue punctuation

- Any other change in style to show a different timeline/perspective is being shown

Character/World Guide

- Full names of all characters (usually in order of

importance, but can be in order of appearance or alphabetical order) and their pronouns, plus any nicknames and who uses those nicknames

- Notes on character voice, e.g. if a character uses specific slang

- Each character's appearance

- Apostrophes for possessives in nouns that are up to interpretation, e.g. *James'* versus *James's*

- Spelling of all specific places, companies and brands that may be used, like the local café the characters go to

Numbers

- Where to spell out numbers (*fifty-seven*) versus where to use numerals (*57*)

- Dates (*23 May 2016* versus *May 23rd, 2016*) and times (*three PM, 3pm, 1500*)

- Measurements in metric or imperial, spelled out or abbreviated (*centimetres* versus *cm*) and the spacing between numeral and measurement (*3 cm* versus *3cm*)

- Ordinal number use (*first, 1st, 1st*)

Exceptions

- Note circumstances where breaking style is allowed for effect, i.e. in a specific character's dialogue.

Again, although it can feel a little overwhelming seeing all these things to think over, I'm sharing them with you for a reason. Being able to make these decisions on your own and enact them throughout your manuscript saves your editor a lot of time, because you'll have done lots of these easy fixes on your own. This can save you money, but more importantly it empowers you to take charge of your own story, because you're taking control of your style.

Exercise: Create your style sheet

For your current work in progress, start going through the list above and thinking about the style you're going to use. Most of it will be intuitive – you'll already be leaning towards certain usages of grammar, capitalisation, etc. – so it won't be as hard as you might think. Create your A-Z spelling list and other sections, and start filling in the blanks based on the conventions you usually use. Remember, though, this doesn't have to *all* be done at once – you can add things as they come up in edits! Don't panic if it isn't all coming to you immediately. Refer to the sample style guide in the 'Resources' if you need guidance. You can also look up other examples online.

Once you've filled in the blanks on what you already know, go through the style sheet and start making decisions on more complicated style choices, for example when to use formatting like italics. Make sure you also add in your common misspellings so you can refer back easily when you're faced with one you aren't sure about.

With your style sheet on its way to completion, have a quick glance at your manuscript to see where you've veered away from consistency. You can look at just one chapter deeply, or do a Search/Find for something, for example the Americanised spelling of a word you've decided to use the UK spelling for. Go through what's been found and replace any instances where you've gone wrong. (Though I caution against using Find and Replace, as this can sometimes introduce errors.)

Do you feel a bit more comfortable with consistency and style now? Are there any interesting style notes that came up for you, that you might not have thought of before?

4

Identifying Genre and Age Range

Definitions

Clear genres and target audiences help connect readers who are after certain books to authors who have published such books.

- **Genre:** The category a book falls under, such as contemporary, sci-fi and fantasy (SFF), romance, or thriller. This can be even more specific if the book blends genres or fits into a genre niche. Consider online book retailer classifications like *Fiction->Romance->Paranormal Romance.*

- **Target Audience:** The main readership of your
book, detailed by traits like their age, gender,
shopping habits, reading habits, and preferred
genres.

Before we get into editing your book ('My god, Poppy,
how long is this going to *take*?'), we need to think about
who you're writing for, because that helps us learn what
readers might want – and that gives us a way to guide
our edits. I want you to start thinking about how your
book will be marketed and sold as early as possible (sorry).
Often you'll be pretty clear on your genre and target audience, but some books are a little more complex – maybe
they blend genres, or are set over multiple generations so
the age group is unclear. For example, if a novel is set over
dual timelines, one being today and the other being in the
1920s, is it historical fiction or contemporary?

Identifying your genre and target audience helps you
understand the specific readers your book is for and what
they expect, what they want, what they don't want, where
they shop, and more. Understanding them helps you edit
your book to ensure it's marketable. Where will it sit

on shelves at bookstores or online? What online store categories will it fit into best (a more complicated decision than you may think)? What keywords describe it well?

You may know that getting a start on your marketing as an author is super important as early as possible. Building an audience for your book – even long before it'll be released – really helps your chances of the book gaining traction and therefore sales upon release. It can also make you more attractive to traditional publishers, because they see you have a ready-made audience to sell to. But what kind of audience are you building? An email newsletter can be great, as can a TikTok account – but are your target readers consuming the kind of content you're marketing with?

A strong understanding of your genre and target audience also helps your editor. Knowing who you're speaking to through your book helps them edit the book in the best way possible, because they'll know what the genre expectations are, as well as what's appropriate for different age groups. A good editor will be able to see where your book will sit in the current market, and be able to make suggestions based on this. (Though I encourage you to do your own market research too.)

What books are like yours?

The first step to understanding the genre and target audience of your book is reading widely and seeing what feels similar. And yes, it's okay that your book is like other books. There are so many stories out there that most books have similarities – tropes, beats, arcs – and that's where genre comes in. People like to read stories that feel familiar, so don't ever feel like it's a bad thing to compare your book to others.

A marketing tactic used by many authors is comparing their book to bestsellers in their genre. Ever wondered why all YA dystopias are 'The new *Hunger Games*' or 'Perfect for fans of *Divergent*'? These are what we call 'comparison titles' or 'comp titles'. They help the book find its audience by letting readers of similar books know they might like this one, too. Read some books that have similar themes, characters, or style to yours. What genre are they considered? How has the genre affected the way they were written and marketed?

Look at those similar books' reviews online (not critical reviews, but those from actual readers, as you might see in StoryGraph or retailer review sections) and see what kinds of readers they're popular with. Is this book a hit on Instagram with 30-year-old women? Or a children's New York Times Bestseller? What made it successful with its readers? Can you identify what marketing tactics were used to reach these readers? Let what readers thought guide you in what they're looking for in new books in the genre. For example, if people didn't enjoy a certain trope in a popular, similar book, you might rethink including that trope in your book. You can also use this in your marketing, with a hook that tells the reader it's giving them exactly what they want, like, 'It's like if *The Hunger Games* wasn't so sad!'

You can pick any comp titles you like for your own use, but when it comes to marketing, be specific and strategic. Don't tell people that your book is 'like *Lord of the Rings*'. That only tells me it's a fantasy – nothing more! But if you told me it's '*Lord of the Rings* meets *Lord of the Flies*' that's suddenly a lot more exciting. It piques interest by telling us what the book is like but also telling us what makes it different.

Be careful, too, of comparing your book to the biggest, best, bestsellers. Telling everyone your book is 'like *Gone Girl* but better' is only making a huge promise you can't necessarily keep. People want to know what to expect, not hear you bragging about how your book is the next big thing – and they especially hate you putting down other books to uplift your own. Be smart!

Where does your book fit in its genre?

Now you've read lots of similar books, you should know your book's genre inside-out. You'll have noticed the things that make books like yours tick, whether it's the types of characters and relationships, tropes and expectations, or the tone. If there's murder it's likely a mystery, if it has dragons it's definitely a fantasy. Basically, each genre sets 'rules' that you can follow (or bend, or twist, but never fully break) to make its readers happy. So, if you're writing a book that sits on the same shelf as so many similar ones, how can you make sure your book stands out to readers?

Picking a popular genre might open you up to a broader audience, but there will be less competition in more niche genres, because fewer authors will be writing in them – though they'll come with fewer readers. It's about seeing what readers of your type of book want and delivering it. Basically, a key to selling books is finding out what a genre is missing and what readers are asking for, then giving it to them. Earlier, when you read reviews of similar books, what did readers say fell short in those books? What worked well? Can you provide a novel that does what a popular author did but *better*? (Subjective, I know, but always worth thinking about as you write.)

While filling a gap in the market can be great, chasing trends usually isn't. It can be tempting to look at tropes that are doing well right now and write to them, but trends come and go quickly. Don't write the dragon fantasy with enemies to lovers now expecting it to be huge when it's finally published in two years. Write the book of your heart, the *book you want to read*, before you write what everyone else wants. If you write about something trending now, by the time you publish, readers could be sick of it.

As always, balance is key. Write what you want with what readers want in mind.

Who will relate to the plot and characters?

If readers don't care about your character's journey, they'll stop reading your book, or never buy it to begin with. You need to know who will resonate most with your story. You can't say, 'But everyone will love my book! It's for all ages, genders, genres . . .' That's simply not how it works. People want a relatable experience that speaks to them, so a generic book usually isn't going to hook anyone strongly enough to be successful. By casting your net too wide, you've missed what was right in front of you.

Think about your book's plot and how readers might relate. What's it about? What kind of people read about the topic you've written? A YA book about a teenager in high school will, of course, appeal mostly to teenagers in high school. But it's more complicated than that. Your subplots will also be important, for example whether your book includes romance.

The main character's age is a great indicator of who the book is meant for. Young people may struggle to read about older characters, and older people may struggle to read about younger characters. Typical age ranges in publishing are:

- Baby (board books)

- Children's (picture books)

- Junior (chapter books)

- Middle Grade

- Young Adult

- New Adult

- Adult

Just by reading the blurb or looking at the cover, readers will decide whether they'll relate to the book or not. If you aren't clear in many ways – your writing, your brand, how you present yourself online – on who your book is for, those specific readers won't find it. Or worse, the wrong readers will find it. A real example of this is the use of 'cartoon covers' in the romance genre. These simplistic illustrated book covers, depending on the art style, can evoke the idea that the target audience is much younger than the content of the book actually follows. This leads to minors unknowingly being exposed to adult content. This can lead to a lot of backlash, which an author or publisher never wants.

To sum up this chapter, although the book is yours, and the first few drafts should be all about telling *your* story, it eventually becomes a product out in the world for people to consume – or choose not to consume. Making sure your book appeals to and is appropriate for your genre and audience is a key part of self editing, publishing, and marketing.

Exercise: Your target reader

A common marketing tactic businesses use is creating a personified target audience 'character'. This helps them figure out *who* exactly they're talking to, and *how* to talk to them. As we talked about above, having a target audience in mind informs more than just the marketing, but the product itself. Entrepreneurs want the products they create to benefit their target audience in some way, so they actually buy it. A product has to meet a want or need, has to fill a gap in the market, otherwise, why invest in it?

Coming up with a persona that represents the target audience helps entrepreneurs make products that will appeal to the people they want to sell products to, and helps marketers talk to those people and communicate why the product meets their want or need. They can really get into their target audience's mindset by using the character as a persona they pretend to speak directly to, which helps them visualise and target effectively.

So, why not do this as an author, AKA someone who's already an expert at creating characters? Remember that you're an entrepreneur and your book is a product. We may be attached to our work as a creative output, but if we want to turn authoring into a career, we have to see our work the same way a businessperson would. This sometimes means altering the 'product' so it meets our target audience's wants and needs.

You can start by creating the character in the same way you would a book character. What's their name? What's their age? What do they do every day? What do they look like? What's their backstory? You can even use the attached Character Building Worksheet in the 'Resources' section of this book. Then we have to get into the nitty gritty that helps us understand who they are, what they want and need, and how to talk to them. This includes:

- **Demographics**

  - Age

  - Gender

  - Location

  - Income

  - Education

- Job

- Family

• **Psychographics**

  - Personality

    • Values, traits, interests, and attitudes

  - Lifestyle

    • What do they want?

    • Behaviours, motivations, problems that need solving, etc.

    • How do they spend their money, and how do they make decisions on purchases?

  - Feelings toward the product (books, or books in your genre)

    • What problem does reading books solve for them? Are they an escape from everyday life? Do they give them a thrill? Do they teach them lessons?

- What do they want in regards to books? In reviews of popular books in your genre/target audience, what are readers asking for more or less of? Where are gaps in the market you can fill for them?

- What challenges do they face in buying books? Are they too expensive or inaccessible? Do they have enough time to read?

  ○ How do you reach them?

    - What social media channels are they using, and how do they use them to communicate about books?

    - Where do they buy books?

    - What are their favourite books?

Bonus: For an A+ on this exercise, now go into Amazon and look through book categories. (You don't *have* to use Amazon, but they often have the most categories to choose from, and they're easy to look through. You could also use the industry standard BISAC categories for this.) Thinking from the perspective of your target audience character, identify which genres they might be looking through for their next read. Go deep into the categories and get as specific as you can. As you identify your sub-genre, look at the top selling books. Can this inform, in any way, how you write, edit, and market your book? Read as many of the bestsellers as you can. Study what they're doing well, and where your book could stand out amongst them, improving and building on what's already been done. Don't forget to look at reviews of those books to see what readers are saying about them.

5

Notes on Structure

Definitions

- **Arcs:** Not to be confused with ARCs (Advanced Review Copies, used in book marketing), story arcs are like bridges. You start at one end, have to climb over, and finally reach your destination. Some bridges are steeper than others, some are smooth, some have rough waters beneath, and some are wobbly rope bridges over deep ravines. A novel has an overarching arc, which encompasses the main plot (again, the major A to B or journey to the destination), and other arcs along the way, including subplots and character development.

You probably have a good idea of what you want to say through your story. Maybe there's a theme or message you hope to convey, or a character you want to introduce to the world. You might have a fictional setting you've loved mapping out, or thought of a storyline you've never seen before. These major aspects are often where novels start. We have a big idea, a 'what if', and start turning it into a story. From there, it becomes a written book, an entire world made up of words on a page – but still, the concepts almost always come before the writing.

We have to make sure those big concepts are nailed down in the structure before we go into copy edits. Our characters need to be fleshed out and relatable, our worldbuilding clear and immersive, and our plot paced seamlessly. It's never a good idea to do copy edits on a book that still needs developmental work. It would be like icing a cake you forgot to bake! It might look okay, but it'll lack substance. Or, the substance won't be very pleasant . . .

My plotting story

When I first started writing, I had no clue at all how to actually write a book. (Not a bad thing – we all start somewhere!) I'd looked into some basic three-act structures and seen writing advice on platforms like Pinterest, or in interviews with my favourite authors, but I had no education and no experience in creative writing. I studied and learned by reading, reading, and reading. I looked at the way characters were written, the way authors crafted prose, crafted worlds, and where the big plot points landed in my favourite novels.

In those days, I hated the idea of outlining. Living with ADHD, it's difficult for me to follow any kind of organisation. At the time, I just wanted to have fun and see where my stories went. Unfortunately for me, I've learned I'm not the kind of writer who can do that with much success. I threw away the first draft of my first novel (*Golden Hour*) and rewrote it almost entirely. Then . . . I pantsed that draft as well, leaving it, too, with many issues. Many, many edits later, I adore that book – a dystopian story following three morally grey teens – and am so proud of all I learned from it, but I don't know if it'll ever be publishable. That's okay! It was a learning curve, and I've come to terms with it being something that's just for me.

It was during writing my second (also unpublished) manuscript *An Enchanted Earth* that I started outlining. I didn't have much of a clue, still, but I had more education (I'd done a creative writing minor at university), had read and studied far more books, and had the experience of my first novel in my wake. I used a simple three-act structure, mapping out what I wanted to happen in each chapter to hit the right beats. Still, it turned out wonkier than I'd have liked. And way too long. The plot, to me, was imperfect and didn't make a lot of sense. But over its many edits, I've come to love that story and its imperfections. Sometimes you write a book that feels like a story you're channelling from another world, and you can't change some things because it would lose authenticity – that was *An Enchanted Earth.* It's a story straight from my heart that I'd still love to publish, but I've come far enough that I know it needs work.

What was most important in *An Enchanted Earth* was having a strong idea of the characters, the main conflict, and where I wanted those things to go. The worldbuilding, magic, scenes, and stakes came to me along the way.

It was still quite pantsed, even though I was following a basic structure. This book was so much easier to write than *Golden Hour*, because I knew what needed to happen and what I was working with. I kept every piece of important information – like how the magic could be used, the timelines, and more – in a spreadsheet that could be accessed easily.

By this point, I'd gone back and created a really strong outlining sheet for *Golden Hour* – because it needed so much reorganising and structural editing that without going through each chapter and outlining what happens, which point of view the story is in (it has three in first person), what is happening for each of the characters, when and where the scene is set, and any subplots happening, the story would have always been a big tangled mess in my head. Oh, what a lesson to learn. This giant spreadsheet I made also had pages on characters: their personalities, looks, backgrounds, motivations, strengths and weaknesses, likes and dislikes, and character arcs. *And* pages on the magic system, worldbuilding, timelines, and more. This spreadsheet became the template I now use for all of my books.

Many changes were still made in the *many* edits that followed for *An Enchanted Earth*. I even changed the gender of one of the two main characters. (Why did I ever think she'd be a guy? But we learn.) Then, during the beta reading process, I found out that some aspects of the story weren't coming across to readers. I changed the stakes in some ways, fleshed out the descriptions (show versus tell was one of my biggest struggles), made the characters and their motivations clearer, and gave them a much bigger showdown at the climax.

Being able to see the entire story laid out in an outline made beta feedback much easier to work with. Without my spreadsheet showing me where each plot point was, it would have been near impossible to see where I could add the necessary scenes/character development. This is why I highly recommend that even pantsers create chapter outlines and character sheets. Even simple ones. It helps you to see the bigger picture of the story and avoid pitfalls like losing track of plots and characters. It won't take long if you do this as you go, but it'll save you a lot of stress later. I know, because this is a lesson I've had to learn myself.

Figuring out the best method (for me)

I can't write this section without shouting out *Save the Cat: Writes a Novel* by Jessica Brody, 2018. This has to be my most recommended writing resource (after this book, obviously, which is *the objective best*). It offers a life-changing method for an author like me who needs a solid outline to avoid letting the story go all over the place. Even if you're a pantser, it's a great book to study so you can learn why certain plot points work best in certain places.

With the *Save the Cat* method of fifteen story beats, I wrote *Woken Kingdom* (my third novel, but first published) in record time. My edits were quicker too, because I wrote a strong first draft by knowing exactly what needed to happen and when. Beta feedback came back mostly positive, because the book was written with a proven method for effective storytelling. That isn't to say you have to do the same, but choosing a ready-made typically-successful method can massively help. As always, there's no real right or wrong – your story is your story.

For my second book, *Cygnus Curse* (Woken Kingdom #2), I used *Save the Cat* again. When drafting *Haunted*

Princess and *Spellbound Empire* (Woken Kingdom #3 and #4) however, I veered away more because the method is a bit more difficult to enact for sequels. But, having the knowledge of how to outline effectively (and where audiences expect certain story beats to be) has allowed me to continue writing strong first drafts that need minimal developmental edits. Keeping the tension up, knowing where an inciting incident goes, and retaining strong internal and external character arcs right up to the big finale, are just a few things having a strong outline can boost for a book.

I've come to love outlining, and find it to be one of the most exciting parts of writing – especially worldbuilding and character creation! I still learn plenty as I write, and change things as I go, but having a foundation is vital for my storytelling.

Now, I'm going to sound like a hypocrite . . . because I've become more experimental with my writing in the past few months, and tried out some pantsing again. When you see my romantic comedy *Laws of Attraction* on the shelves in a couple years, that's what I'm hinting about here! Even though I wrote it without a detailed outline and wanted to simply see where it took me, draft one was still pretty successful compared to my previous pantsing attempts. That's because now, even without in-depth out-lining, I subconsciously know where the story needs to go – and how to get there. Once more, it's foundations, practise, and learning that are the keys to growth as an author.

Where can *you* start?

I've shared my story to help you understand that every-one writes differently, and that your methods can evolve over time. It's important to always experiment and find a groove that works for you. Even the most meticulous plotters will make changes as they edit their work. If we aren't always analysing what's working and what isn't, and trying different ways to make the story engaging, we aren't really editing. That means the first step in book structure self editing is looking at the major aspects of your story with a developmental editing eye.

Ask yourself some initial questions to get an idea of your plot, such as:

- What's the main conflict?

- What goal, need, or passion drives the main character?

- How does the main character fit into the setting?

- How does the main character develop throughout the story?

- What's already been done in the genre, and in what ways is your story unique?

- What are readers of this genre asking for? Do you meet genre expectations?

Now, consider how all of these story aspects might fold into a novel structure with a beginning, middle and end. There are many structures out there that you can follow, but to keep it simple (because in this book I'm teaching you how to edit for structure, not write from scratch) let's look at the basic three-act structure that most stories follow. Keeping this in mind as you edit will help you put your story beats in the best places. However, never feel boxed in to following a specific method – if you can do your own thing well, then go right ahead! This just helps us meet the standards readers expect better, giving us a higher chance of success.

Beginning

The first part of your novel is all about introducing your characters and conflict. This is where a reader will decide if they'll continue or not. If they aren't intrigued now, they might put the book down. We have to edit it to utterly engaging, riveting perfection.

When editing the beginning of your story, you'll want to analyse how you're giving readers the information they need to understand the story. Are you weaving information into the story, slowly revealing things through conversations and conflicts? Are you using flashbacks to explain the background information readers need to know? Does the way you present information draw the reader into action and excitement, or does it feel like reading a textbook before you can get into the actual story? (Hint: Look out for the chapter later in this book on first pages!)

The beginning has to both create mystery and answer questions. Within the first ten pages, the reader needs to be totally hooked. They should already feel an emotional connection to the main character – such as wanting them to succeed, pitying them, finding them funny, wanting them to survive, or any other way you can make the reader root for them. You also need to have given just enough contextual worldbuilding and background information that the reader can understand what's going on (but not in an exposition dump – we'll come back to this later).

In the beginning section, focus on what's normal for the main character. Then, what's the inciting incident that flips their everyday life on its head and launches them into the plot? Rather than the reader feeling as if they've been dropped randomly into the character's life, it should feel clear why the story is starting where it does. If your beginning section lacks this 'launching', it may not be effective and you'll want to look at editing it.

Middle

By the middle of your novel (which should begin no later than 25%, or readers may start nodding off), the story is in full gear. Your characters will be developing, chasing after their goals, and new information and plot twists will occur to progress the plot. This is the journey, the huge chunk of the book that has to lead us from the beginning to the ending.

For some authors, this is a journey a hero needs to take to confront a villain. For others, it could be a character getting through the school year and finally taking a big exam. Maybe they're getting to know their love interest, so they can finally declare their love for each other at the end. It's all the ups and downs that happen to get a book from A to B. Lots of writers get lost in the middle of the book, but the middle *is* the book. It isn't filler. It's the biggest part, where readers spend the most time. You have to make it count.

Whatever it is you make the middle of your story about, the journey must be interesting, emotional, and purposeful, and include several minor conflicts and subplots to keep the reader engaged. It's easy to start losing your way and letting the tension drop, padding out scenes with filler to bulk up the word count. This is not an effective way to tell a story. Each chapter should add more and more tension, snowballing until you reach the ending.

In the middle, you can also include a strong 'midpoint' where a major conflict occurs, along with a plot twist that changes the direction the book is going in. This doesn't necessarily mean an absolutely huge twist, like making a romance novel turn into a sci-fi horror (though I guess you could, if you really want to). It's about moving around the stakes, challenging the characters' beliefs, and introducing new problems for them to face. If they've so far been on an upwards spiral, their life getting better and better (say, they've discovered a portal that takes them to an amazing magical world), a twist can come in to make things darker. Or, on the other hand, if everything has been going wrong for your main character, you can give them a win that gives them a pick-up until the ending where they're knocked right back down (before finding a happy medium). In *Save the Cat,* this plot-twisting strategy is referred to as the 'false victory' or 'false defeat'. It's a super helpful way to keep the story engaging.

We should also talk about subplots. Within your main story arc, you'll have several subplots that keep your audience engaged, building throughout the story. Your subplots could be a bit of romance, an underlying mystery that needs solving, a task that the main character needs to complete, or any other plotline that's separate from the main story but still relevant. Subplots are great for keeping your readers engaged through the middle section of your book, as they'll create the smaller conflicts and climaxes. They can also be a great space to explore side characters and expand the story.

If your middle section feels like filler rather than authentic, tense, progressive *story*, engage in some developmental edits to make sure each chapter is really adding something to the plot and character development.

Ending

Now you're at the end of your novel, the final 10-20%, in which we have the finale – the major climax and the subsequent resolution. Does your main character win the battle? Do they find happiness? Or is it a tragic ending, in which they die or lose someone they love?

It's usually best to have a wrapped-up, satisfying end for your characters. The reader will want to feel like they've earned something after reading your book (even if the ending is sad, they should have a sense of completeness), and not like they've missed out on something, or read an entire novel just for a major conflict to remain unresolved. It's a bit different if you plan to write a series, but even then, enough should be wrapped up that the reader is satisfied more than dissatisfied.

You'll also need to consider if an epilogue is needed. Many authors add this final bonus chapter at the end to show their characters after the conflict is resolved. How are they dealing with their changed lives? Epilogues aren't necessary, but they can be a good addition. Just remember to not end the story too late and keep it going on and on. Once the final battle is won, in whatever form that takes, write 'The End' and get it done. An early exit is better than a book that drags.

When editing the ending of your novel, make sure all the conflicts and subplots feel resolved in a satisfying way. The finale should be tense enough, and the characters should have worked hard enough to reach their goals, that the ending really pays off. If the end lacks tension and feels more like a slow ride off into the sunset, dragged out unnecessarily, consider reworking it to retain engagement and excitement right to the last page.

The Internal Story

While it may be tempting to focus entirely on the external plot, in which conflicts and action are happening, it's equally (if not more) important to have an internal plot that follows the growth and emotions of the main character.

Stories aren't just about the adventure your character is thrown on. They're about how your character *changes* throughout the story. This growth, becoming who they really are and who they're meant to be, is what makes them human and relatable. What's the big lesson they learn? Do they become a better person, or a worse person? This is what you probably know as 'character development'. Without this internal arc, readers will find it difficult to root for your main character, and therefore even the most exciting, action-filled external plot can feel empty.

Internal and external arcs can also be known as the 'B' plot and 'A' plot, which mirror each other. Something external happens, and the character reacts internally, changing in some way. Something internal happens, and the character's emotions affect the world around them.

Things that happen to us in real life affect the way we think and behave – whether it's a big traumatic event or an innocent comment, our outer world impacts our inner world. And, after an internal shift, our actions change and therefore our experience in the world does too. Just like in reality, it's vital in fiction for these two arcs to intertwine to create a story that's both engaging in action and emotionally charged. This keeps readers hungrily turning the pages, invested in finding out what happens next.

For writers who are naturally quite character driven, the plot may be mostly happening inside. Rather than an adventure with a clear endpoint, or a mystery to be solved with clues interspersed precisely through the story, these novels may have a heavier focus on how the character changes. Most books will lean one way or the other and be more plot or character driven – but in edits, make sure there's a good level of balance. Neither the internal nor the external story should be massively overshadowing or weak.

As part of your character information sheet (which we talked about under 'Style Sheets'), you can track how your character changes throughout the story. This includes how the writing needs to change as the story goes. For example, if your character starts out shy, and they hunch their shoulders and bite their nails, those mannerisms have to be replaced as they gain confidence. You may even choose to create two information sheets – one for the character at the beginning of the story, and one for the character at the end. Some authors even use line charts to track growth, showing at which points the character is their best, strongest self, and at which points they fawn back to their weakest. If there are multiple main characters or timelines, these all need to have the same considerations – every character should change in some way and *be affected* by what's happening, while *actively affecting* what's happening.

Bringing it all together

Now we've looked at the major parts of a story – beginning, middle, end, and the internal arc – let's look at how to put these ideas into place. Here's an example three-act plot for a romance novel:

- **Beginning:** Jill is afraid of romance after a nasty

breakup. She's lost confidence in herself, and doesn't think she'll meet the right person. Her best friend says she'll find her soulmate eventually, but Jill doesn't believe it.

- **Middle:** Despite Jill's refusal to see it, her new next-door neighbour is majorly crushing on her. They're a perfect match, and get to know each other over their shared love of gardening, chatting over the fence.

- **Subplots:** Jill is also struggling at work, but with a new work friend, she relearns some confidence. She's going for a promotion, and her budding romance distracts her, but ultimately the romance and friendship she's found give her the confidence to grow in her career as well.

- **End:** Jill finally realises her neighbour might be right for her, and lets herself enjoy the relationship that's grown from their friendship. She has a new lease on life and believes in love again.

- **Internal Arc:** Jill has gone from a shy person who doesn't see love for herself into a confident woman who achieves her goals and dreams. She knows now that she's worthy of being loved by the people around her.

Here, the romance is the external arc, while Jill learning to love herself again is the internal arc (or character development). Both of these arcs are important, because the romance helps her learn to love herself again, but at the same time, regaining confidence in herself is what allows her to accept love into her life. The subplot about work and a new work friend gives her more depth and mirrors the main story, teaching Jill lessons she can carry into her romance. The ending, of course, is a happily ever after.

As you give your book a structural edit, keep an eye on this basic structure. All books have a beginning, middle, and end, so this is universal and natural to include in a book. It might just need some tweaking to ensure the tension stays up. No matter what you do, the most important thing is analysing how effective each section is. If you feel the engagement falling off anywhere, or the external and internal arcs feeling disconnected, there may be some developmental changes to make.

Exercise: Match your story's A plot to its B plot

If you've already written or outlined your novel, use it for this exercise. If you haven't yet, or if you'd prefer to play with a new idea, feel free to make something up! It's always good practise to try something different.

Create a timeline for your A story (external arc) that has a beginning, middle, and end, and fill in the blanks of the main beats it includes (including the subplots). Create a separate timeline that tracks the B story (internal arc) from the beginning to the end. Put the timelines side by side. Do they intersect and impact each other? Can you match up each beat with a moment of growth, where the character either matures and becomes more themselves, or is pushed back in their growth journey? Can you identify how their internal state affects their decisions, and therefore the plot?

When you look at the timelines you've created, do they feel realistic and match up, or are things a little messy? Are there clear beats in both the internal and external stories? Based on your findings, is the story more character or plot driven? Does your character have enough agency, making their own decisions, or are they passive and thrown around by the plot a little too much?

6

Realism: Making it Feel Authentic

Let's go even deeper into developmental edits! Like the structure of the novel, the aspects that make it feel 'real' – like worldbuilding, characters, timelines, pace, and voice – are important to nail down before you get into the copy/line editing stage. You can edit a book that's missing realism, but it would only be a Band-Aid when the book might need surgery.

When I'm discussing realism in the context of fiction, I'm not referring to facts and figures (though that can be part of it). I'm also not talking about making it feel like real life, because then we wouldn't have sci-fi and fantasy, and all their subgenres. What I *am* talking about is a holistic approach to writing that makes the book feel like it's truly happening – not just being explained to the reader – and therefore evokes the right emotions and gives readers the best reading experience.

It doesn't matter if you're writing a complex fantasy novel with magic far beyond our reality, or a contemporary based on real-life settings and day-to-day occurrences. Books either do or don't feel 'real' to readers based on the way you build and tell your story. That means even books with dragons and magic, or time travel and spaceships, should feel like they're really happening as the reader consumes the story. The reader should feel so engaged it's as if they're right there, not constantly pulling back and grumbling, 'As if that would ever happen!'

You might have heard about the concept of 'suspending disbelief' when we're being told stories. Different people have different levels of what they can and can't accept in fiction, but in general readers can still be absorbed into a story even if it has wildly unreal concepts. This is an amazing thing our minds can do! The suspension of our disbelief allows us to escape into amazing worlds and stories far from what we'll ever experience in reality. We can imagine, create, and enjoy the most far-fetched epic fantasies or faraway planets. We can immerse ourselves in romances that are one-in-a-million in real life, or follow the story of a detective with superhuman smarts. And it feels so real it's like it's happening to us.

There's a trick to pulling this off, though, because we can only suspend our disbelief *so* much. Finding this balance between the real and unreal is a major aspect of writing amazing stories that fully engage readers. **In fiction, we make everything we can as realistic as possible, to increase our trust and authority in the eyes of readers, so that the unrealistic aspects are believable.** Over the next four chapters, we'll be talking about worldbuilding, characters, timelines, and voice, so you're empowered to bring full depth, emotion, realism, and atmosphere to your novel.

7

Thorough Worldbuilding

Whether your setting is a high fantasy empire or a familiar town from real life, your story exists in a 'world'. And the fun part is, you get to craft it! Worldbuilding includes 'mapping out' your setting both on a large and small scale, from the fictional realm or real country your novel is set in, to the more personal physical spaces your characters find important (like their home, workplace, or favourite cafe). The stronger your worldbuilding is, the more the reader will be immersed in the story. With a high level of depth and atmosphere in the world, your readers will feel as if they're really there – which is a huge part of the 'realism' we're looking for.

You might be writing a fairy tale land with magical creatures and talking trees. You might have an alien planet that isn't at all like Earth. Maybe the entire story stays in one place, just one room, or house, or spaceship that the characters are stuck together in. Regardless of how *out there* the setting we're dealing with is, readers need to feel immersed. Not just from the description of how it looks and feels, but from realistic factual aspects – like how long it takes to get from the east coast to the west coast of a desert island.

When describing the world/setting, use all five senses. Don't only tell the reader how it looks, but really show them how it *feels* to be there. It isn't like a regular movie, but a 4D immersive experience. What's the weather like? Does your main character's bedroom smell like their favourite candle? Is their workplace climate controlled and bright, or is it a dark, hot factory? Using all the senses is also a great way to weave setting and description into the story instead of 'exposition dumping' it. Show your reader the setting during the action as your character experiences it. Don't tell us the candle smells good – show us how the character enjoys the specific scent.

Thorough worldbuilding goes a lot further than the five senses, though. You need to know your setting's culture, history, terrain, layout, and more. (Check out my Worldbuilding Worksheet in the 'Resources' section of this book!) For your story, this might mean establishing timelines for a monarchy, knowing the climate and culture of an area, or creating the name, menu, and layout of your main character's favourite restaurant.

When you edit your book for worldbuilding, there are so many things to keep in mind to make sure it's understandable and immersive. Let's look deeper into worldbuilding by discussing place, time period, culture, issues and dangers, magic systems, and how your character fits into the world.

Place

Where's your story set? This is the most obvious part of worldbuilding. We have to know where the characters actually are, physically and geographically. Real world settings have different expectations than fictional settings, so let's first look at how they differ, and what you need to keep in mind for both.

Real-world settings

If your story is based in the 'real' world, you'll need to plan out the area your character lives in, and any other areas the story takes place in. You might have chosen a setting that already exists for your book: a big city like London or a holiday destination like the Bahamas. If so, you'll need to make sure you've researched the place very well, either by travelling there yourself and taking notes, or by listening to others' experiences, like by looking online for questions answered by locals on sites like Reddit.

A very quick way to alienate readers and shoot your realism right in the foot is to get something wrong about a real place – especially if it's a place a lot of people have been to or call home. For example, if you say that hopping in a New York City cab and going from the Empire State Building to the Met Museum takes about the length of your character's short phone call, but it's actually a longer trip due to traffic, your readers could be very offended.

(Offended may seem like a harsh word to use for this, but people do get very picky and patriotic about their hometown. They won't be shy to leave a negative review for such a faux pas!) Similarly, describing a hot afternoon at the beach on a lovely summer's day in Antarctica will pull the reader right out of the story. This is the last thing you want to do, because the reader should always be fully immersed, not pulling away to go, 'Huh?'

That said, you *can* invent parts of the world, for example a café the character goes to that doesn't actually exist. As long as you aren't specific (for example by giving an address where something else exists and there couldn't possibly be a café) this is believable enough.

If your setting exists in our world but isn't a real place, you get lots more wiggle room – but also the responsibility to balance the realism with your inventions. Once again, even a small town in Antarctica that you've made up is probably not going to have a hot summer day. This may seem like an exaggerated example, but readers really do care about these things. Even if they don't get up in arms about you making an error about how warm it is in December in your made up Spanish town, they can often sense the lack of authenticity subconsciously and it affects their reading experience.

What about urban fantasy, magical realism, or para-normal?

When we have magical aspects in a real-world setting, the reader is suspending their disbelief already. In this case, there's often more room to make things up. Since the reader already believes there's vampires in Sydney, they can also believe in a hidden vampire den below the Opera House. Whether you make things work because of magic, or find a way to fit unrealistic things into the real world logistically, the reader can typically believe changes made to the real world. This concept can be carried over to 'portal fantasy' books, in which the character starts in the real world but finds themselves in a fantastical world; there's likely to be some magic bleeding through into the real world, so it's okay to utilise your readers' suspension of disbelief.

Fictional settings

If your story is set in a completely made up, fictional world (as is often seen in sci-fi and fantasy), you'll need to go even deeper. You're inventing not only a country or town, but possibly a whole planet yourself. In the realm of science fiction and fantasy, readers are open to a lot of things, but once again, they can only believe so much.

Many new high fantasy authors are tempted to use a generic setting, with a blank-slate Medieval Europe, Arthurian type of world that doesn't have any specific culture or terrain, but definitely some dragons and wizards. Similarly, worlds of the Fae are tempting to writers as they're extremely popular right now – but because of this, many writers follow basic formulas and don't build out their world realistically. While this lack of individuality and specificity can be comfortable for readers since it's so familiar, it also shows a lack of creativity if that setting isn't fully drawn-out.

Be cautious of relying on generic settings and letting readers fill in the gaps themselves rather than giving them a full immersive experience. Stay in control of your own story and use the five senses to show how your character moves through your magnificent world.

Editing setting

When editing a story for realism at the setting level, specifically the physical space the character occupies, an editor will be looking for strong realism that creates so much atmosphere it's hard to put the book down and return to real life. They'll do some fact checking too, including making sure you're right about it taking three days to travel by horse from your character's home village to the kingdom thirty kilometres away where their big quest will end. They'll check that you're right about the flowers you described being in bloom when your main character and their love interest meet for the first time. They won't check every single thing, since they can't realistically be expected to, but an editor will usually have a broad range of knowledge and know when something seems off.

To self edit your setting, make sure you can answer questions like:

- What country is the story set in (fictional, real, or fictional based on a real place)?

- Where in that country?

- What does it look like? Smell like?

- What are the buildings like?

- Is it a lower or upper class area? (How is this shown?)

- How do people travel, and what do people do for fun?

- How's the weather?

You also want to consider nature and terrain, and how they affect the world. Is the setting a dry desert, or a tropical island? A story in either of these places will be vastly different. When doing your developmental editing, keep a close eye on how the physical space interacts with the plot. If something is missing – maybe it's too generic or confusing – make some edits and look at how you can expand the depth of your settings to affect what happens in the story more.

If the character is often moving about their world, it can also be very helpful to create a map. Either draw one yourself or use a program with free and paid options, like Inkarnate, to help you visualise the geography.

Time

When is your story set, and how does this affect the plot and characters? We know society has changed so much throughout human history, even just in the last hundred – or even five – years. Every period in history and across our world has its own culture, fashion, and language. The same can be said of fictional worlds, which should also have clear timelines for realism.

Whether you're writing a historical romance or a futuristic dystopia, you want to do the research to make sure the timing adds up. This means looking at the historic time period to make sure your facts are straight, or making sure the timelines are realistic for your future world to make sense. And don't forget that timing plays a role even in books set today. Let's look deeper into time period as part of realistic worldbuilding.

Timelessness

If your book is set today, or even two years ago, you can hit a bit of a speedbump when it comes to aiming for timelessness – that is, if timelessness is what you want. Some writers do love to have a clear slice of life in an exact year, or try to make their book as up-to-date and relevant as possible. That means making additions such as current slang and technology, clothing trends, or references to specific movies or celebrities.

Many authors, however, want to go for a more timeless feel. It would be incredibly difficult to make a book feel like it could be happening any decade, but you can set a book 'now' that feels timeless and can be enjoyed for longer without it becoming dated. To do this, the trick is to avoid specifics that would put the book in a specific year. For example, to write a book set in the late 2000s-2010s, you might mention smartphones but not any specific models, or social media but not any specific apps. You wouldn't reference particular movies or celebrities unless they're iconic across generations, for example, *Titanic*.

I see a lot of authors struggling with timelessness, especially in the traditional publishing world. Let's say you're trying to write a current trend into your book, like the latest TikTok dance, so you can appeal to a young adult audience. By the time the book comes out – often at least one or two years after being signed, because trad publishing is *very* slow – the trend is pretty outdated. That means readers will feel thrown by the reference, pulling them out of the story. Your fun, up-to-date addition ends up having the opposite effect of what you intended. This is why, in general, I caution against specifics if you want to have a timeless book that can be enjoyed for many years.

Where does your story fit into your world's timeline?

It's also important to look at where your plot fits into the history of the world (real or fictional). Is the plot set after a war that changed society? Have the people only recently developed technology? Has magic been hidden or forbidden for centuries to only now start popping up again? Basically, how does the world's past impact its present, and what will happen in the future?

If the history is important, it can be a great help to create a world timeline (hint: timelines can also be great for the plot of the book and where it fits into that history). This is especially important if your book spans multiple generations. When it comes to editing, if your timeline is quite complex, your editor might create a timeline themselves as they go – similar to a style sheet (or even as part of the style sheet) to ensure everything is landing in the right time and place.

You do have to make sure you keep on top of these things when editing, because readers are really good at catching timing plot holes, especially if they're well-versed in your genre. It can get you into a lot of trouble if you're merely guessing timelines and throwing in plot points without properly thinking it through. This is okay when you're in early drafts and still figuring things out, but as you edit, make sure timelines are very clear and realistic.

Culture

The societies within your world might be just like real life, or might be unrecognisable. Either way, you need to know how your characters interact with and are impacted by culture. To write a realistic world, you need to know the special customs of the people you're writing about, how the government works, if there are religions, what the expectations are in society for different kinds of people, and in short, why things are the way they are.

- If it's a **real culture** you're writing about, especially if the culture isn't your own, make sure you do extensive research and engage sensitivity readers to ensure you're writing about it appropriately.

- If it's a **fantasy world** you're building, which may have different cultures within it, make sure each culture is properly fleshed out so it makes sense to and engages the reader. Be cautious of relying on harmful stereotypes if you're basing fantasy cultures on real cultures.

Within the culture part of worldbuilding, consider:

- Architecture

- Religion

- Slang

- Fashion

- Arts

- Technology

- Food

- Multiculturalism

. . . And literally anything else you may think of that helps flesh out the world and make it your own!

On your first drafts, you may be focusing on getting the story down and not so much on creating a world that has a lot of depth in its society and culture. As you move into later drafts, start to fill in the gaps where you can and keep notes of the choices you've made so you stay consistent.

Issues and dangers

The problems your world faces might be the driving conflict (or external/A plot) of your story, or may enhance it.

These issues and dangers can be anything from monsters, dangerous terrain, and dystopian governments, to more localised/everyday problems like bullies at school, a toilet paper shortage (god forbid – I can't do that again), or gentrification. Issues and dangers in your world may mirror problems our real world faces, like we see in dystopian fiction.

But don't give your world a lot of issues and dangers if they won't affect the story. If there are lions living in the mountains by your fictional city, are they a threat? Has your main character dealt with them before? Will they actually appear in the story? If not, they probably aren't worth bringing up. We don't want to confuse the reader with useless information and overcomplicate things – though sometimes a couple of red herrings that distract from the true problems *can* be fun.

Dangers in the world can be a great subplot. The main character might need to navigate through an ocean filled with mermaids to reach their goal. In this case, it's a great addition! Especially if the mermaids end up coming back later, bringing the plot point full circle.

If the big issue or danger in your world is a major driver of the story – say magical storms ravage a small village, and the main character goes on a quest to break the curse that makes the storms happen – you'll want to give it a lot of thought and depth. How long have the issues been going on? How have they shaped society today? How have they shaped the main character's life? Bringing all these things together is what makes the story a story, and the world a fully realised one.

Magic systems

This one's just for our sci-fi and fantasy authors. Some books in other genres might have aspects of magic, such as some supernatural elements, or some technology different from ours, but they likely won't have the same level of complexity. While fantasy books have magic systems, sci-fi books have what I refer to as 'technology systems'. These systems dictate what kind of otherworldly or unreal aspects are included in a novel that falls under any of the many subgenres of SFF. High fantasy, urban fantasy, dystopia, space opera, cyberpunk, paranormal romance, just to name a few.

When it comes to realism in your systems, possibly the most important aspect is the limits and rules. While magic systems are pretty limitless, technology systems tend to be more science-based. So, to edit for realism here, we have to get really clear on exactly how these special elements in your book work. Remember that making your world as realistic as possible helps the reader believe and engage in even the wildest unreal concepts as they read, allowing them to suspend their disbelief.

There are two main types of systems: flexible systems that aren't overly detailed (*soft*), and rigid systems that have very detailed rules and classes (*hard*). Whether you use a soft or hard system, it's important to at least go into enough detail about how things work that the reader understands what can and can't be done. This is integral to the plot, because if the system is so flexible or so much is possible that someone or something becomes too powerful, we start to lose tension. Whether the plot is around stopping a supervillain, aliens, vampires, or rogue magic, why worry about the big bad when everything can be fixed with the wave of a magic wand?

This is why we have our rules and limitations. They help us and the reader make an airtight plot, where they can't be pulled out of the story by wondering, 'Why didn't they just use a spell to light their way through the dark tunnel?' or 'If they can shapeshift, why not use this ability to trick the villain and defeat them more easily?' Setting a limitation that stops the magic or technology being overpowered to the point of losing tension could look like:

- The main character can read minds, but only when making eye contact with the other person.

- Everyone is born with magic, but it's illegal and needs years of training to successfully use, so not many people can actually do anything with their power.

- Robots can do almost anything, making them the perfect workers – but the government has total control of them.

- Everyone on the planet has a hovercar, but they can only go a metre or so high.

Here are some questions to get you on the right track when building and editing a magic system:

- Are people born with the ability to use magic, or

do they obtain it?

- Is this ability internal (magic comes from the person) or external (magic comes from an external source but is wielded)?

- Do training and skill impact the level of magic that can be used, for example a 'master' being able to do more complex or stronger magic than a 'novice'?

- Do different people have different amounts of magic to use?

- Are there different types of magic within the magic system? How do they interact?

- What can the magic be used for?
  - For example, psychic abilities, telekinesis, attacking power, or elemental power.

- What does the magic look and feel like?

- Does using magic take a toll on the user or have some sort of cost?

- What are the limitations of the magic? What can it not do?

For technology systems, it's more about the science feeling realistic even if it's very out there compared to what's currently possible. Maybe people have super-powers, but how do they obtain them? Maybe they're travelling in light-speed spaceships, but how do these work? You don't need airtight answers – we're writers, not scientists! – but once more, you need to explain things enough the reader can believe it *could* happen.

How does your protagonist fit?

We did it! We created a fully realised world! Now, this is the most important part. You have your setting ready, but how does this come together with your plot and characters? Your main character needs to have a purpose in the world you've built. Maybe they're going to rebel against a corrupt fantasy queen, maybe they've just moved to a new city and have to navigate it, or maybe they're saving their small town from being bought by big developers.

What will your character do to change the world, or what will happen in the world to change the character? Just like how the internal and external story arcs are intertwined, the physical space your character occupies should be deeply linked to the story and feel lived in – which means establishing an emotional connection via the characters.

This not only includes watching the world change through their eyes but seeing how their perspective changes. If, at the beginning of the story, they're unimpressed by most things and depressed, they might view their space as dull – but by the end, if they've found a new lease on life, they might describe things vividly and with excitement. Does the world around them cause them to harden or soften? What do they do to change the people and places around them?

Final note on worldbuilding: Don't do too much

Although you need to know everything about your world, the reader doesn't – and especially doesn't want to be told it all at once. Readers can quickly become bored and fatigued with long descriptions of things that aren't relevant to what's happening to the main character 'now'.

Stick to introducing parts of your setting *as needed*. Readers are not here for a history or geography lesson – they're here for a story. What's actually important right this second? And as you give description of the world, consider what readers can infer on their own. For example, instead of telling us the protagonist's room has four walls and a ceiling, tell us about what posters they like to put up, how neatly they live, or what colours they like. These manners of worldbuilding are significantly more powerful and engaging.

Exercise: Create a village

Worldbuilding can be really fun, and it doesn't even have to be part of a novel. Lots of people create whole worlds as a hobby, or even part of games, with deep lore, terrains, and magic. It might even be a happy place you escape to in your imagination! To practise worldbuilding, play around with different settings, build out different places with characters, cities, monsters, and more. But most importantly, just enjoy the process of it.

For this exercise, I don't want you to plan a whole world, but a small village or estate. Under different headings, map out:

- The layout of the village

- The climate

- The time period

- The characters, e.g. a baker, a hairdresser, a farmer, etc. and their dynamics

- If there's any magic in your village

- If there are any issues or conspiracies

- Brief notes on the culture

- Sketches and drawings, if you're so inclined

Then answer some of these questions:

- What's the most important thing to the people of the village?

- What do people do on a rainy day compared to a sunny day?

- If someone from a totally different walk of life stepped into the town for the first time, what would their impression be?

- Are any of the villagers fighting with each other?

- Is there a secret the villagers are keeping?

- What's the best place to get a cup of coffee?

This can be fun on its own, but you can also take it a step further and try to write a short story with what you've come up with. You might even use this world to practise outlining a novel. Again, you don't have to write it, but just enjoy playing and broadening your skills.

8

Characters with Depth

Definitions

- **Main Character (MC) or Protagonist:** This is the person the book follows most closely, and in most cases, the book is in their Point of View (POV) so we see the story through their eyes. It's their novel, and they have the most impact. A book may have more than one main character, but there's typically one that leads.

- **Love Interest (LI):** In romance books, or books with a romance subplot, the love interest is usually the second most important character. They interact the most with the main character, and there is a romantic tension between them that's likely to end up in them having a happily ever after.

- **Antagonist:** These are personified roadblocks to your main character's goal. They can be anything from a bully at work to a supervillain – but what's most important is they both mirror and oppose your protagonist.

- **Secondary Characters:** These are also important characters, appearing as 'helpers' who drive the plot forward or help the main character in some way. They might be the main character's friends and family, coworkers, people they meet along their journey like mentors, or more.

- **Side Characters:** Like extras in a movie, side characters tend to show up no more than once and have very little impact on the plot. However, they're sometimes needed to fill a scene. For example, when two characters are on a date at a restaurant, they'll need a waiter. But even if the waiter has dialogue, we typically don't focus on them much, and probably don't name them or describe them, because it isn't important for the reader to know.

Oh my gosh, this is my favourite part and I'm so excited! You have an amazing world that you've edited to have real depth and atmosphere, and now we get to start filling it with characters. But, of course, there's no proper order these greater aspects need to be done in. In fact, you're likely already ahead on your character creation, especially if you have a draft or two down. For many writers, characters are the first part of the story they come up with, coming to them as a concept before the world and plot are even thought of. It's only natural. As people ourselves, it makes sense that the people we write into our books often come more easily than other aspects.

Although we may be drawn into a story because it has the premise of a steamy romance, fire-breathing dragons, or a high-stakes thriller plot, what keeps us reading and what makes us emotionally engage with a novel is its characters. They aren't mere props to throw around. They should feel real so readers can empathise with them and care what happens to them. They should have agency in the story, making their own decisions and reacting appropriately to plot points, *and* have a strong development arc from the beginning to the end of the novel.

As you go through each draft of your book, you'll want to see how you can expand each character's personality – whether it's by clarifying their background, making their unique voice stronger, ensuring their actions align with their values, or checking they develop across the story. There's always more to uncover about your characters, and getting to know them better is a big part of the fun of editing.

Sadly, not all characters are created equal. Often, writers rely on stereotypical characters, or characters without agency and emotion. To be clear, what does it mean when people say a character is one-dimensional? Simply, it's a character that feels *flat*, like a piece of paper – a caricature rather than a fully-realised person. This might be okay for a side character, like the shopkeeper who sells your protagonist oranges in chapter four then never shows up again. But when it comes to your main and secondary characters, they must have *depth*.

Strong characters have a range of positive and negative traits, unique to their distinct personality and past experiences. A hero shouldn't only have good qualities, and a villain shouldn't only have flaws – that would make for a pretty boring story. The best protagonists have relatable flaws and difficulties to face, and respond to the events in the story appropriately. How do we create this depth and realism? Let's get into it.

Character arcs

As we talked about under 'The Internal Story' earlier in this book, the arc of a character (internal plot/B plot) is as important as the external plot (A plot), and the two should be entwined. A stagnant character doesn't inspire readers. There's a reason people love redeemed villains – they're exciting, and easy to root for. You empathise with them because of how far they've come.

On a smaller scale, how can your character grow throughout the story? What lessons can they learn, and how can those lessons be relatable to readers and draw empathy from them? You might start with a character who's shy and believes they can't express themselves authentically, but over the course of the plot, they're pushed to make big decisions and get out of their comfort zone. They learn to love who they are and become more confident. Alternatively, a character who is initially grumpy and unlikable might learn through new relationships to be kinder. You can also have negative character arcs that work well, like villain origin stories. The point is that either way, the character grows into their true self and as they change and develop, they become better equipped to deal with the main problem or villain in the story. This helps craft the super satisfying resolution readers love.

Personality

Now you've conceptualised your character's arc in your story, you have to figure out how to show their personality and development in the story. A hot-headed character will act very differently to a meek one. Their personality will drive the story in many ways, as it will change how they interact with the conflicts that occur. Because the character should fundamentally change between the beginning and end of the book, we have to effectively understand why they need to change, how they're going to change, and most importantly how to narrate this.

Remember the rule 'show don't tell' (which we'll talk about more later in this book). As you edit, try to rewrite where you've described a character's personality with phrases like 'He was very shy.' Instead, show the reader that your character is shy through their actions, like having hunched shoulders or a quiet tone. In a realistic book, a character's personality should be obvious through their body language and dialogue.

When thinking of personality, try to avoid obvious character archetypes and stereotypes like the strong hero man or the mean popular girl. These are extremely tired, and people are often no longer interested in reading about characters that aren't unique and relatable to them. Look at the 'why' behind the things your characters do, and look at ways to make parts of their personality conflict in interesting ways (for example, they're a musician, but they have stage fright).

Background

Where does the character's personality come from? Just like how you have to deeply know your worldbuilding even if most of it never ends up on the page, you need to understand all the ins and outs of where your character comes from – their life story and how their past impacts them today. As you edit your book, some of this will become more apparent and you'll get new ideas. In general, try to answer questions like:

- Where are they from?

- Did they grow up in a city or small town?

- What's their family dynamic like?

- Have they dealt with oppression or adversity?

- Have they dealt with trauma?

- What's their life like now compared to their past?

- What has happened in their life to impact how they act today?

With these answers, go back through your book and assess the character's personality. Does it all add up? It can help to do some research into psychology and truly understand how someone's past can form their present actions. For example, someone who's dealt with lots of bad breakups might have given up on love, or someone who grew up poor might now be very frugal. Someone who was abused by their parents might be very insecure, while someone with loving parents might be a little too naïve.

Editing to ensure a character's background comes across clearly and impacts who they are now brings stronger emotional connection, as readers can understand why they are the way they are. This is one of the most fun parts of realism to work on, because you get to fully create a life story!

Wants and needs

Your main character's desires will be one of the strongest drivers of your story. What is it that they want or need? How does their drive to achieve this goal create conflict? How do their wants and needs change as they learn lessons, obtain new information, and their circumstances change along the way? And most importantly, how can you as the author prevent them from reaching these goals?

Some characters just do good because they're good people, but others need a stronger motive. And this more complex motive often makes for a more interesting story. I always love to talk about how well Katniss Everdeen in *The Hunger Games* (Suzanne Collins, 2008) is written. She was never interested in saving the world. Her only goal was to protect her family. She wasn't a hero and had no desire to be one, but was thrown into conflict because of a single choice she made to save her sister, which spiralled into being the face of a revolution – something she never wanted. This made for a very interesting character arc; this complex characterisation is a big reason why the series is so successful.

When editing, make sure each character has a purpose and reason for every action they take throughout your book. Even if they're very archetypal, you have to know what made them that way, and there should be some growth by the end of the book. Although sometimes we're on autopilot, most things we do are to reach some sort of goal – be it in our love life, career, financial state, home life, social standing, or more. Your characters should be led in the same way. And remember, inaction is also a choice a character can make. Avoidance and denial are just as interesting as action, as long as the character isn't passive.

Strengths and weaknesses

There's so much room to play here, creating movement and tension through each character's strengths and weaknesses, and how these impact the plot – just like how wants and needs do. I'm sure you've thought a lot about your own strengths and weaknesses. How have they affected your life? A character should be just as driven and impacted by theirs, which is why, through each edit, we draw these out and make them a shiny, impactful story aspect.

A good balance of strengths and weaknesses is important for any character to have. A one-dimensional character with only good traits isn't going to interest readers, because being perfect isn't relatable. We can't root for someone who has everything, unless their story is a fall from grace, because if they have no problems, where will the tension come from? They need to have flaws – even a fatal flaw – that makes them someone we can see ourselves in. Alternatively, a character who has too many flaws, or is too weak or passive, will bore readers. Agency is vital to make us want to follow someone's story. If they never make decisions, never go against the grain, and everything happens *to* them, they're hard to root for.

As you edit your book, look at how your character's strengths and weaknesses affect how they react to the plot, or *cause* the plot. Do they have a solid balance of strengths and weaknesses? Do these strengths and weaknesses make sense in terms of the character's background (e.g. they grew up poor, which manifested as a strength for saving but a weakness with financial anxiety)? Do they change throughout the book as the internal arc impacts their abilities?

Physical appearance

If you're someone like me who loves visuals and aesthetics, then you've made it to the fun part. Although they say you shouldn't judge a book by its cover, nor a person based on their appearance, a character's looks are usually the first impression a reader gets. The way someone presents tells us a lot about them – and the way you weave this description into the story is important, too.

The basics, like hair, skin, and eye colour are all important, but readers will be more interested to know about little things that make your character unique. This might be a scar, or a certain item of clothing they always wear. It could even be their level of grooming; a well put together character will create a different image than one with less hygiene.

As always when it comes to description – which we'll discuss more later in this book – it's most effective to intersperse it through action and use all five senses. This creates more vividity and assists the reader's memory, as opposed to explaining everything about a character all at once. Maybe they're a chef, and as they reach for a pan, their perfume can be smelled over the food. Maybe the first glimpse we get of their wavy chestnut hair is when they take off their helmet after bike riding.

It can also be helpful to reiterate appearance occasionally to strengthen the image in the readers' mind, but don't underestimate them. Too much description will bore the reader and possibly stop them from reading on. (How many books tell us about the love interest's 'ocean blue orbs' over and over and over and . . . You get it.) Make it interesting, engaging, and *relevant*. If you're struggling to think of unique description, there are countless websites that offer ideas.

Characters in conclusion

I could talk about characters all day, but this chapter should really be about editing and improving your work, not creating characters from scratch. If you want more, though, I've shared my full Character Development Worksheet in the 'Resources' section of this book. It has a huge list of questions to consider about a character, which will help you make sure they're written with full depth – from their looks and mannerisms, to their background and development arc.

Here are some more fun ways to train yourself to craft more realistic characters:

- Read widely, including non-fiction (such as memoirs) to get into the heads of real people on the page or characters others have written.

- Listen. So many of us are poor listeners, and we don't fully engage in conversations. Truly paying attention to not just what people say but *how* they say it, and what the *subtext* behind what they're saying might be, teaches us how other's minds work and how their personalities are expressed.

- People watch. Take time to observe how different people move around and use their bodies. If possible, get out of your usual spaces to expose yourself to people and cultures you aren't always around. How do they dress? How do they walk? What kind of body language do they use?

Exercise: Create a character sheet – of yourself

How would you describe yourself and tell your story if you were a book character?

In a format of your choosing – a spreadsheet, document, blank piece of paper, or a template like my Character Worksheet – create a 'character' of yourself. Start with physical aspects like your appearance, body language and mannerisms, and style. Then go into some detail on your personality, your likes and dislikes, and your positive and negative traits. You might also include your background or some core memories, events, or traumas that have helped make you the person you are. Add in your day-to-day life, like your job, where you live, your family structure, and hobbies.

Are you learning anything about yourself yet? With this next prompt you might, because a character isn't just a list of traits – they're fluid and have development over the course of the story. So, I want you to pick a period of time in your life, such as the last year, or the transition from childhood to your teen years. What were some major events over that time? What did you learn? How did you change and evolve? Did you perhaps become a better or worse person?

No, this isn't a therapy session, but I want you to get into the mindset of how people change and why it's so important to include that development in the characters in your stories. That's how we get realism and relatability! You could also use this exercise to practise character creation by making character sheets of your friends and family, or even make up an entire backstory for a person you only briefly met. I encourage you to practise this as much as possible, learning to pay more attention to the world around you so you can apply it to your craft.

9

Realistic Flow of Events

When do the story beats happen in your novel, at what pace, and how do they impact the characters? As an editor, an issue I often see is writers throwing lots of action or traumatic experiences at their characters to create drama, but failing to see those experiences through. Realistic timing in your novel is about making sure each scene is purposeful to the plot, to the characters' development, and makes sense in the overall timeline.

To help you understand what I mean, here are some examples of poor timing:

- In action stories, when many traumatic events, like fights, aren't fleshed out enough, and the characters get over them too quickly (e.g. healing from physical wounds faster than possible).

- In romance, when two strangers become inseparable and fall in love far faster than is realistic or makes sense for their characters (known as 'insta-love').

- In quest, adventure, or travel stories, when characters move between locations unrealistically quickly/slowly (which is also usually a worldbuilding problem!).

If you don't have a timeline of the events in your novel – not an outline, but a chronological list of events including things that happened before the 'now' of the story – now's the time to make one. With this in front of you, you can carefully consider the pacing of your novel: when things happen, how long they happen for, and how much of the story (how many words) they take up. Which timeline events do you want to deep-dive into and lengthen, and what can be skipped over to get to more engaging or important plot? For example, we can skip the characters' school day, even though it takes up most of their day, to get to the exciting magical plotline where they fight dragons at night.

Your character's internal arc also needs to have a realistic flow. This means that while they change throughout the story, sometimes they go backwards in their growth and make mistakes. There should also be a good balance of the character having agency and shaping their own story, and them being influenced by the plot points that happen to them. Remember that sometimes things happen to us that are so traumatising even the strongest of us can't be heroes in that moment – this humanity makes for great emotional connection in your story. Development should always feel human, because that's the reason we put it there in the first place.

Let's leave this chapter on the shorter side, since we've already talked enough about plotting! The main takeaway here is editing for realism as you draft, checking that each event you excitedly wrote in the first draft makes sense for the overall story. If you're unsure, you can always talk it over with a friend or critique partner to see if something that makes sense in your mind also makes sense to others.

Exercise: How long is this going to take?

Let's use an example of something your main character goes through that you've also been though to look at how realistic your story is. For this exercise, pick something that happens to the main character in your story that's either based on your real life, or that you've had a similar experience with. Whether it's recovering from a broken ankle, hitch-hiking from Los Angeles to New York, getting over a break-up, or falling in love – what's an event that inspired your book?

Create a timeline based off your novel of your chosen event – the start to finish. (If you haven't written the novel yet, or would rather try this with a different work in progress, just play with a possible timeline and reuse this later for your outlining.) Then, create another timeline of how it played out in your real life experience.

For example, you might choose the timeline from receiving a bouquet of flowers to the point where they start to wilt and then are thrown away. In your book, how is this timing spread across the story? And in your real experience, if you've had flowers given to you, can you remember how long they took to begin wilting? You could even go and buy yourself a bouquet as research to watch how long it takes and practise observing realistic timing. (But do not do physical primary research on examples such as breaking your ankle, please!)

Now you have both timelines of events, match them up and see how realistic the story version is. Does your main character run twenty kilometres across the city to save their love interest's life far too quickly? Do their home renovations take a lot longer than usual for no apparent reason?

Even though sometimes we can shift realistic timelines a little to serve the story, it's important to retain realism as much as possible so the reader can stay engaged. How do your timelines weigh up? If they don't match, how could you add or remove time or even plot points to make it more believable?

10

Editing for Structure and Realism

We've talked a lot about the bigger picture now, and all the elements that go into a well-structured, fully realised book that readers will be deeply immersed in, both hitting the right beats and surprising the reader in fresh ways. In chapter one, we talked about the steps of creating a book, particularly the importance of doing several drafts and editing in stages. Remember that your first few drafts shouldn't focus too much on perfecting the prose itself, but on these bigger-picture ideas we've been discussing in regards to structure and realism.

This is why I recommend first doing a full read-through of the book prior to *any* edits – but not before putting it aside for a little while. Whatever stage you're currently up to, resist the urge to start editing too soon. Instead, let your mind wander to different things. Forget about the manuscript as much as possible. This is a vital part of getting space from your writing so you can come back to it with fresh eyes. The more you've let yourself forget about the story, the more you'll get to experience it like a first-time reader – which is the headspace you want to get into so you can make the most informed edits.

The problem is, you know your story inside out, left and right, upside down. If there are gaping plot holes, or huge lapses in necessary information, you're often going to miss them. Giving yourself a few weeks or months away from the story allows you to see where your all-knowing author brain forgot to fill in the gaps. Because, sometimes as authors, we know our story so well we forget to actually *tell* it!

Once you've had some space, do your full read-through. You can do this on the computer, read it as an eBook (by turning the file into an ePub – this is my favourite method), or print it out. Keep a notebook at your side as you read, and take notes of:

- Any places where the pacing feels rushed or drags

- Where tension falls off

- Where characters act out of character

- Where a character's motivation is unclear

- Characters that don't serve enough purpose to take up page space

- Subplots and arcs that are left unfinished

- Scenes that don't add to the story/build tension

- Scenes where too much is happening

- Exposition dumps

- Missing information

- Where the voice isn't strong/isn't 'in character'

- Where your voice changes and doesn't fit the novel (which sometimes happens if we're reading other books and subconsciously take on other authors' voices)

- Plot points that seem too easy/deus ex machina

- Plot points that feel cliché

- Character emotions changing too quickly (e.g. an enemies to lovers romance happening unreasonably fast)

- Character arcs feeling out of place/not working

- Where you lose interest

- Where you feel less emotionally connected

- Where the worldbuilding is confusing or lacking

- Any new ideas you come up with

- And anything else that comes up that you think you want to change!

At this point, again, don't do any actual editing. Don't worry about the grammar, how it sounds (except for overall tone), description, show-don't-tell – none of the sentence level stuff at all. I know, it's hard to ignore. Chances are these aspects *won't* be great at this point, but we don't need them to be. There's absolutely no point getting caught up in these aspects if you're going to rewrite the scenes for structure anyway. Again, that's why we do structural edits first and line-level edits second.

So now you've finished the read-through and made all your notes, think over the story as a whole. Is there anything else you want to change, now you can see it from a wider perspective, like:

- Character arcs that didn't work

- Worldbuilding that needs improving/clarity

- Chapters/plots to discard entirely

- Chapters/plots to enhance

- If the beginning, middle, and end sections (or however you've divvied up the beats) feel balanced or if you need to add to or take away from the word count.

Taking your notes from the read-through, you can then go back into your chapter outline and highlight where different edits need to be made chronologically. You can also create a master-list of edits to keep in mind in each chapter (for example, changes to a character's personality, or wanting to overall add more description).

If you don't have a chapter outline, now's the time to make one. Yes, even if you're a pantser and hate outlining. That's only for draft one. At this point, you have to make sure all the puzzle pieces fit, and a strong outline is vital for this. (Have I gone on about this enough yet to convince you?) There are many ways to do your chapter outline, but my method is to have the following columns in an Excel spreadsheet for each chapter. Even better, since you're already doing a re-read, you can create your outline as you go – it isn't as hard as it may seem, I promise! Here's what I include:

- Chapter Number

- Date/Time

- Place/Setting

- Chapter Summary (very brief)

- Subplots/Arcs included

- Character POV (and their character development in the chapter)

- Any other characters that appear (and any notes on their development)

- Word Count

- Cumulative Word Count

- Other Notes

- Ideas for edits to make later (in the next draft)

Follow the link in the 'Resources' section to download the outlining template I use, along with an example based on my novel, *Laws of Attraction*.

Once you have your outline, notice how it allows you to pinpoint where things are happening, find sections easily, and keep track of subplots and character arcs. Once you copy your notes in from your re-read into the 'ideas for edits' section for each chapter, your long list of changes to make is going to feel much easier to work through. You can then do your developmental edit chapter-by-chapter (or in whichever order you prefer – this is just my method) making everything more seamless and simple.

Exercise: First five chapters

Let's not put too much pressure on just yet. For this activity, I want you to outline only the first five chapters of your book. If you already have an outline, I still recommend trying this activity for the sake of using a different technique and seeing what new information presents itself to you.

Set up your outline in whatever format you like, but for this activity use the headings I suggested above. Start filling in each section, making sure the outline clearly shows everything that's happening in each chapter but in the *smallest amount of words possible*. This makes the outline easy to navigate. (Hint: this is a great way to improve your ability to write a synopsis, which will come in handy especially if you query.)

You might have some strong reactions as you practise writing this mini outline. You might be having lots of fun with it, already identifying things about your story that you weren't aware of before ('These two characters are together a lot – maybe I should expand on their relationship!'). Or you might be tearing your hair out with frustration, absolutely loathing the process ('Poppy, how dare you try to box me in with some stupid outline!'). Maybe you just feel *whatever* about it – it isn't your favourite, but you know that getting it done is worthwhile.

Wherever you're at, I want you to identify how you're feeling and connect it back to what's flowing and what isn't with my outlining headings. It's awesome if my method works well for you. You can steal my template, fill it in, and tick that box on your to-do list. But if it isn't working for you, that's fine too – we all have our own process. Although I'd caution against throwing away outlining entirely, you can play around with it to find a method that works better for you. Maybe a super simple timeline is all you need, or maybe your outline needs to go into lots more depth, especially if you have a complex world and lots of arcs and characters. Discover *your* way!

Also think about what's relevant to your story. You might add or remove columns based on the information neces-sary for each chapter and the flow of each arc. You could even have a separate column for each arc, a column for the magic system and how it develops, or even how the reader learns about the worldbuilding as the story progresses. There are so many great ways to outline, and there's no wrong way. Have fun and make the process easier for yourself.

11

Chapters, Sections, and Paragraphs

Congratulations! You now know how to structure your plot as a whole, and can go back and complete developmental edits to improve the bigger picture aspects. That means the next level is the chapters and paragraphs the book is broken up into. We're still in structuring, but now on a smaller scale. This is our first step down the editing funnel – are you thrilled yet?

As an editor, I've had several writers ask me how to create chapters. This always stumped me, because for me, chapters have always been intuitive. They start and stop where it *feels* right. This is just one way all writers differ, and something I've had to learn the technical side of so I can help all authors, even though I innately know what to do. Things that are easy for some are mind-boggling for others, and as an editor, I have to know how to explain things in a helpful way rather than simply saying, 'Well, *I feel like* this would be better if . . .'

And that's why I always hammer in the importance of writing your way, and continuing to learn. I don't want to teach you my way as the 'right way', but rather help you find your own method and voice. More often than you may think, writers will write an entire draft of a book but not split it up into any sections. They then come to me asking what to do. Although using chapters, sections, and paragraphs might seem simple to some of us, there are different ways to break up your story. Some authors may even choose not to use chapters at all. So, it's okay if you're a little lost on what you want to do.

My first piece of advice, which you might not like, is: if you want to be good at structuring your chapters, sections, and paragraphs, you need to start by reading widely and studying how other authors do it. Just like with every other part of writing. We study, study, and study, and we use what we pick up on to find success in our own work.

Reading is what helps us understand how authors put the things I'm teaching you in this book into practise.

But of course, I do have *real* advice for you here. Like always, let's start with the biggest aspect (chapters) and work our way down to the specifics (paragraphs).

Effective chapters

How can we define 'chapters' in fiction? Again, it may not be as simple as you think. Chapters aren't just scenes, and they aren't the author breaking up the story however they feel like it. The choice of how chapters are laid out is one that takes a lot of thought, because they're integral to the reading experience.

Here's how I'd define chapters: **A section of your book that can be any length and cover any scene/s, but is purposeful in giving the reader breathers and building tension.**

In general, we change to a new section or chapter when the storytelling changes, or when we want to create some kind of impact. That might mean moving between scenes, a time skip, a location change, movement to another POV, pausing to give a cliffhanger effect, or a similar moment of impact. Remember, a chapter is not a scene, and it does not need to cover everything that happens to a character from the start to the end of an event. Telling the reader everything from the moment the character wakes up to the moment they go to sleep is an ineffective way to write. Your chapters should start and end *in the middle of the action*.

Let's take a phone call, for example. Have you noticed how in books and movies, the characters often don't say 'hello' and 'goodbye', or participate in any small talk? The dialogue jumps right into the topic, like, 'Stevie, he kissed me! What do I do!' Even though this may seem a little strange to us, we already know how a phone call starts and ends. In a story, we have limited time. We want to get to the core of what a conversation is about rather than waste page space on everyday things that can be assumed. Skipping everyday non-story is not only an acceptable break of realism but a highly effective one.

Similarly, you wouldn't call emergency services and start with, 'Hello, how are you?' You'd jump straight in and say, 'Please help, I think I'm having a heart attack!' This skipping to story-related plot is also why characters never seem to use the bathroom – unless there's plot going on in there. This concept is the exact same when it comes to your chapters. Starting a chapter in the action and leaving on a cliffhanger is a key to getting readers to not put the book down. While chapters are effective when they each have some sort of arc that makes them make sense as a segment, what's more important is keeping up the tension and energy, and building that tension and energy with each new chapter until the climax at the end. *Boom.*

How about an example of a story where a teenager finds out she has magical powers and is trying to understand where they came from? If we're in a middle section chapter, this is how it could be laid out:

- The girl is testing out her secret powers to see what she can do. The chapter begins as she's already experimenting. (NOT at the start of the day or as she's getting ready, unless that's somehow important.)

- As she tests, she learns more about the magic, but it also brings up more questions.

- Someone walks in. She stops using her magic just in time and manages to hide what she was up to.

- The person hands her a letter and says, 'It's from your great-grandmother. She said you'd want to read it when you turned sixteen.' The girl replies, 'But she died years before I was even born.'

Notice how we don't let her read the letter, nor ask any more questions? That's what we can start with in the next chapter, which the reader is now more likely to read immediately. They want to know what the letter holds, since it likely has to do with the girl's magical powers (how could the great grandmother have known to write it?). And they want to know *now*. Or, if they're deciding to put down the book and have a break from reading, it'll stick in their mind that they want to jump back in as soon as possible.

Remember, by 'cliffhanger', we aren't talking about something absolutely earth-shattering or life-threatening happening right before the chapter ends in every single chapter. Your character doesn't have to end up hanging off the edge of a cliff (but depending on the genre, they certainly can). It's more about opening a question that now needs to be answered, like we did with the letter.

Maybe your character has just had a haircut and dye, and you end right as their salon chair is turning around to the mirror for them to take a look. Maybe it's suddenly started raining while the love interests are out on a date, and they have to run for cover. Or, maybe we *are* going for the classic, big, action cliffhanger, and the character ends up on a battlefield with someone lobbing a sword right at them. The idea that is the reader has to be on the edge of their seat and question, 'What's going to happen next?'

With all this said, the chapter cliffhanger is just one method. It's very hard to get your chapters 'wrong'. Really, it's up to you how you lay them out! Although using cliffhangers is a great technique, you don't have to do every chapter this way. Many authors prefer to have a chapter to a scene (e.g. letting the teenage girl read her great-grandmother's letter, then moving on once that's wrapped up), with chapters like little boxes that tie up each event in the story neatly. The chapter may have a beginning, middle, and end, like an episode in a TV show that has its own arc but is still part of the overall story. This is just as valid, and it's often what we default to when writing, because it feels more natural. I certainly do, but I'm experimenting with more cliffhanger endings to help build tension in my books.

Let me repeat: there's no 'wrong' way to do chapters. They can be any length and include as many sections as you like, so don't get too caught up in getting them 'perfect' – perfect doesn't exist here. At least, every story's version of perfect will be different. Some books work best with long, winding chapters that draw in the reader and don't let go. Others, like action novels, might use shorter chapters for the effect of faster pacing. Often the best is a mix of both, which gives the reader some variety. Too many short chapters or long chapters can be fatiguing.

You should do what feels right for you, and once you get feedback, you can always restructure. Remember, though, that all readers have different preferences, so you can't please everyone. Once again, you need to discover what works best for the story you want to tell. And that's what editing is for. If the story seems to move without any structural flow, with lots of things happening but no breathers for the reader, or it starts too early and ends too late in each scene, consider how you can restructure your chapters for stronger engagement and rhythm.

Chapter titles

Chapter titles should be considered wisely, because they have the power to either add to a novel or to unnecessarily take up page space. Many books will simply use numbers, going from Chapter One, Chapter Two, etc. until the end (this is the current trend). But of course, some authors like to use chapter titles, and this is especially common in children's and middle grade books.

Chapter titles can add novelty, humour, or set the scene. For example, in *Percy Jackson and the Olympians: The Lightning Thief* (2006), author Rick Riordan opens the first book with the chapter title: '*I Accidentally Vaporise My Pre-Algebra Teacher*'. This immediately sets the scene for a book that's filled with action and humour, and tells us the approximate age of the main character since we know he's in middle school. Riordan's use of chapter titles is iconic, and his books are huge bestsellers because he's able to tap into his target audience's emotions so well.

On the other hand, some authors like to use more vague titles that might be a word or two and hint at what we're in for, helping to craft the vibe or theme of the chapter rather than spelling out what it includes. For example, 'love', 'destruction', 'flowers', 'war', or 'ice-cream'. These can be poetic, but if you're going to do this, make sure each title serves a purpose and the words aren't there just to look pretty, which is often the case.

For some books, it makes the most sense to have factual chapter titles. If the narrative follows a strict timeline or is written in diary entries or letters, each chapter might be a date and time rather than a number (a great example is Heather Fawcett's 2023-2025 'Emily Wilde' series). Or, if the book includes a lot of travel, like a quest novel, it might have the location as the chapter title.

Chapter titles can also be used to tell us whose POV we're in, particularly if it's a first person, multiple POV novel. Usually, authors will put the character's name below the chapter number/title as a subheading. This helps alleviate any confusion when switching between different viewpoints, which can be unclear particularly when the voices aren't distinct.

Title case

While we're on the topic of titles, let's quickly go over the options for capital letter use. It can be confusing when Sometimes You See Titles Where Every Word Has A Capital, and Others where only the first word has a capital. Are you ready to hear something mind boggling? As long as you remain consistent in the case you use for titles, it's fine. (I lied about it being mind boggling.) Pick one way to do it and remain consistent, or if you're working with a company that has provided a style sheet, they'll usually tell you their preferred style. Here are the options to choose from:

- **Title case:** The first word and all major words (like nouns, verbs, and adjectives) have a capital letter, but minor articles (like *a*, *and, or,* or, *the*) don't. For example: *The Best Day Ever,* or, *Lover of Paintings,* or, *Betsie Likes the Movies.*

- **Sentence case:** The first word has a capital letter, but any other words except proper nouns do not, like a typical sentence. For example: *The hotdog John ate,* or *Has she gone insane?* or *We try to* *find the best sushi in Japan.*

- **All caps:** More of a stylistic choice, all caps puts every letter in the title in capitals. For example: *SATURDAY'S ANTICS.*

- **Small caps:** Another stylistic choice, small caps in typography makes the letters after the true capitals the same height as lower case letters, even though they're styled as capital letters. For example: *THE STRANGEST OCEAN.*

Effective section breaks

A section break's magical power is linking two sections that *could* be chapters, when you want to keep them together so the 'vibe' can carry through. Just like we can time skip with a chapter, section breaks work amazingly to help us move through the 'boring bits' of a story. They can be used to switch POV, move forward in time, or move to a new location without starting a new chapter.

Basically, it tells the reader that a scene has either come to a close, or you're looking at it from a new perspective.

If they go from one paragraph to the next without a scene break, but suddenly it's tomorrow and the characters are on the moon, they're going to feel super whiplashed – but with section breaks, they know to expect something has changed.

Let's try an example:

Sophie sips from her coffee cup and ponders. Should she accept Jared's offer to take her on a date? The cafe is as loud as her swirling thoughts. He's a great guy, but at the same time, he's never seemed like boyfriend material.

'Order for Sophie!' calls the barista. Thank goodness, because she was nearly finished her first coffee, and she's going to need lots to get her through today.

Jared types at his desk in his home office and feels sick to his stomach as he awaits Sophie's answer.

'What should I do, Mum?' he says into the speaker phone.

'It's alright, son,' comes her crackly voice. 'What's meant to be, will be.'

Did you feel whiplashed at the start of paragraph three? I did just writing it! Without any kind of indication, we're currently in Jared's house and in his head. This jumping pulls the reader out of the story immediately. That's why we use section breaks to ease them into the narrative change. Is this version better?

'Order for Sophie!' calls the barista. Thank goodness, because she was nearly finished her first coffee, and she's going to need lots to get her through today.

///

Jared types at his desk in his home office and feels sick to his stomach as he awaits Sophie's answer.

You can use what we cutely call a 'dinkus' – a symbol, symbols, or even a graphic – to show the section break as I did above, or you can simply use a line break. You take away the indent on the first line after, because it's the first line of a new section (just like we do at the start of a new chapter), and it's that simple!

Section breaks are also used by authors who don't want to use traditional chapters but still need to break up the story. For example, Donna Tartt's *The Secret History* (1993) only has three chapters across its 500+ pages, but that doesn't mean there's never a moment to breathe. The author uses section breaks so there's still a place to comfortably stop reading at least every once in a while.

While section breaks are a great tool, be cautious not to use them as an excuse to skip around too much. Too many sections with short word counts can be jarring and awkward to read. Like with all writing techniques, use section breaks with discernment so they can work well, rather than over-using them to the point of fatiguing the reader.

Chapter and section checklist

Regardless of how you decide to break up your story, each scene should drive the story forward. Your main character should learn something, grow in some way, or be challenged through every scene in the story. We don't do filler around here! Ask yourself:

- Does the scene start in the middle of the action?

- Does the scene serve a purpose in the overall arc of the story?

- Does the main character experience character development?

- Does the scene drive the story forward?

- Does the scene build tension?

- Does the scene have any characters who don't need to be there and could be omitted?

- Does the scene have any dialogue that's redundant and could be removed?

- Does the scene end too late, after the action is done?

- Does the end of the scene make the reader want to keep reading?

Exercise: A day in your life

What's something you recently experienced that turned into a story you've told lots of people? Maybe it was a run-in with an ex at a cafe, a ghost sighting that scared your pants off, or an unexpected gift you received. If you were to write what happened as a chapter or section, can you think of where you'd start, what you'd skip, and where you'd finish?

Here's an idea of a fictional day, crossing out everything I'd skip if it were in a novel:

- ~~I woke up to my alarm, yawned and went back to sleep for a while since it was the weekend.~~

- ~~Later, I got up, had a shower, and ate breakfast. I was excited because today I'd be going to a concert.~~

- ~~I got dressed in the outfit I picked yesterday and called my friends to let them know I was on time for them to pick me up. As they drove to my house, I did my makeup and filled up my water bottle.~~ *(Are you yawning yet? I am.)*

- My friends arrived, and in the car we played the band's music. ~~We found a carpark quickly and hopped out.~~

- We got in a really long line, but we were very excited. ~~We had some sandwiches I packed for lunch.~~ The sun was still strong so I put extra sunscreen on while we waited to enter the venue. But just as I had it all over my face, the drummer of the band came right near us! He was saying hello to fans in line, and my friends were already taking photos. I'd also managed to smear my lipstick while applying sunscreen, so I wasn't just rubbing my face like an idiot, I was covering myself in red.

- I didn't realise until the drummer saw, laughed at me, and my friends made me take pictures with him. I was blushing, but you wouldn't have seen it through all the lipstick. He was so gorgeous, and I couldn't have been more embarrassed. My friends knew I'd had a crush on him forever!

- ~~He left, and I was about ready to cry with shame. At this point, the line was still long, and I really needed the toilet, so I left my friends and sulked~~

~~over to the portable toilets. Once I'd been, I got back in line and we entered the venue, finding our seats. I'd managed to fix up my makeup a bit but still felt very embarrassed.~~

- When we got to our seats, a security guard came up to us and said to come down to the VIP section! The drummer requested us specifically, and wanted us to have a free upgrade after my unfortunate incident. Security told us he felt bad for laughing at the 'pretty girls'.

- During the concert, the drummer kept pointing his sticks right at me, and at the end he leaned over the stage, motioned me forward, and took my hand! He gave me one of his sticks, and I still have it.

- ~~Afterwards, we got in the car and had dinner, then went home. My friends couldn't believe it, and I immediately called my sister to tell her as well. I was really tired but very happy with the day.~~

- ~~I had a shower and went to bed.~~

What I've crossed out here is everything someone I'm telling the story to wouldn't need to know. If I went on about what I had for breakfast, it would take forever to get to the best parts. It would be like telling a joke that takes five minutes of talking just to get to the punch line. Audiences get bored quickly when they're inundated with useless information. Unfortunately for me, in real life I'm very much a rambler. I tend to over-explain everything and spend a long time waffling before I get to the point. That's why I know this can be a big learning curve for authors.

For this exercise, write out everything that happened in one of your favourite stories to tell about yourself – start to finish, including the boring bits. Then, cross out everything that isn't necessary to the story, just like I did. You can be brutal. After you've skipped parts, think about formatting it like a book. Would you use section breaks or maybe create a new chapter, or would you continue through the story?

Effective paragraphs

Hel*lo*, this is our first look into the copy-editing side of things! We're really edging out of the bigger picture concepts and narrowing down. But before we get deep into your prose, let's look at your paragraphs and how they're laid out. Paragraphs tell us when we're moving from one concept to another – moving to a different character's dialogue, moving onto a new topic, a new thought, or more. They're great for clarity and allow us to create some rhythm as we write.

Many newer writers struggle with this, and aren't sure when to move to a new line. It's okay – it's not too complicated, and you'll get there with practise! There aren't many hard rules on paragraphs, except to move on for clarity, and always move to a new line for a new speaker in dialogue. It's all about flow and readability. So, the best advice I have is to think like the reader and consider where moving to a new line will help their experience and understanding.

Just like how sections and chapters exist to give the reader breathers, paragraphs are a great way to stop readers getting fatigued as they read. Since it's more of a design concept, many writers might not have thought of this, but the use of formatting – white space, particularly – is a great technique for retaining the reader's attention. Too much text can look like a giant block of *blergh.* We use the blank space on the page to make the writing more consumable and easy for the eye to run over. Remember – too much white space can be tiring, too, so as always it's about balance. As we edit, we want to take notice of how much white space is on the page versus how much text, and if we can format our paragraphs in a more balanced, readable way.

Paragraph length

Long paragraphs (typically a paragraph that goes over ½ of a novel page) are a huge chunk of text that's hard on the eyes and the brain (remember, *blergh*). Especially these days, with our ever-decreasing attention spans – especially if you have ADHD like me – lots of long paragraphs can be grating and exhausting. They might be so much effort that the reader stops reading entirely because the book is too tiring to get through.

That isn't to say you should avoid long paragraphs at all costs. It's about variety and never too much of the same thing. Long paragraphs can be great for monologues, description, a tad of exposition (just a tad!), or as a way to really keep the reader held in an emotion/moment. Meanwhile, short paragraphs are fantastic for speeding up pacing and building tension. We can absolutely use a mix of both for the best effect.

Moving between short, medium, and long paragraphs works so well because it keeps the reader more engaged. Variety in a novel makes reading feel like a dance rather than a marathon. Remember – reading is a physical thing. Your eyes are moving around and taking in information. As you move through your book and edit on this level, see if you can identify places where there's too many long or short paragraphs, or where some breaking up or blending could really add variety and enhance the reader's experience.

Exercise: Where are your paragraphs?

We'll keep this exercise simple. Take a single page out of your manuscript (or if you prefer, from a published book you like) and study where each paragraph sits. What choices have you (or another author) made in regards to paragraph placement? Where does the story tend to move to a new line?

Consider, broadly, the scene this page is set in. What's most important here? Are we in a fast-paced, high-stakes scene, or delving deeply into the character's emotions and inner monologue? As mentioned above, we can use paragraphs to invoke certain feelings in the reader, so I want you to think about how you tend to use your paragraphs and what effects you're creating. You might even ask a friend to read the page aloud to you, to gauge how well the paragraphs pace the scene.

Learning where you naturally break is a great way to start improving and using paragraphs strategically rather than randomly. Of course, many paragraphs will be based on dialogue, character, or theme. But there are more ways we move through our story than you might first think.

12

First Pages: Introducing the Story

The first page of a novel is likely the hardest you'll write. Before we get into the writing itself (are you sick of me stalling yet), we're going to get this extra tough starting point out of the way. It's so easy to get stuck here, so let's *un*stick. With the massive task of hooking the reader, introducing the main character, stakes and setting, creating an emotional connection with the reader, *and* setting up the story to follow, getting your first page right can be overwhelming, but it's absolutely vital. Unfortunately, this is where many newer writers go wrong.

When you're telling someone a story, let's say catching up with a friend for dinner and chatting about your day, it's pretty natural to begin by setting the scene. You might overexplain things, giving a long description of the setting, what the people involved looked like and what they were wearing, what the weather was like, and context from other days and times to make the event make more sense.

In a novel, this often doesn't work. We've already talked about how important it is to start in the middle of the action, drawing the reader in right away. We don't need to overdo the telling and give them a play-by-play of the entire day just to get to the punchline. There's no better way to lose a reader than to make them wait for something interesting to happen. It's kind of like when you're going for a swim but the water is cold. You can either dive right in and adjust, or you can go inch-by-inch, slowly trying to get yourself used to it. You're much more likely to freak out and give up if you go in slowly, right? Although diving in is scarier, it's often the better option.

Captivating readers works in the same way, and although this advice is great for every scene, it's never more important than on the first page. This is the first impression –

the part a reader is glimpsing when they pick up the book in a store or library, pick it up out of their to-be-read pile at home, or when they read a free sample of the eBook. They need to be engaged immediately and want to keep reading to make that *yes* decision. If they're met with a big block of text that provides lots of context and explanation but no story, they're probably going to put the book back and find another one that excites them more. And for a harsh truth, there are plenty of books out there for them to choose from, so if you've already lost most readers from page one, the book might not stand a chance.

So, how do we captivate readers right away? *Action* and *emotion*. Something needs to be happening, and the reader has to care.

Readers don't need all the context right away – and especially not all at once – to connect with a story. In fact, dispersing information throughout the first few chapters works better, since it adds an air of mystery and makes the reader turn the page to better understand your world. They can dive in and comfortably adjust to the water, rather than get in reluctantly, toe-by-toe, every second thinking about running back. This dive in is the action and emotion that immediately tells them what the vibe of the book is and who the main character is. From the very first line, they're launched into the story, into the mind of the narrator, and they want to know what happens next. Not because they have all the context, but because they're emotionally connected to the main character.

Consider these two opening lines:

1. *In the magical world of Fairyland, it was rainy and cold, so all the elves had raincoats on.*

2. *The Master Elf was about to yell at Marlene, and she knew exactly what magical scheme she was in trouble for – but how could she have resisted?*

Which one makes you want to read on more? While option one situates us in a fantasy world and gives us an idea of the weather, it tells us absolutely nothing about what the story will be about. Option two tells us nothing about the world we're in, but gives us an exciting idea of who the main character is, and has us asking questions right away. What did she do to get in trouble? Why couldn't she resist? How much trouble is she in?

Option one isn't 'bad', but it doesn't offer the same level of engagement. To retain the original idea but improve it, we could make it something like: 'Marlene pulled her raincoat's hood over her pointed ears and sighed – it was as if someone in Fairyland were using magic to push bad weather her way on purpose.' This version gives us an indication of whose story we're following and that it's in the fantasy genre. She also seems to have a bad attitude about the weather, a victim-like mentality that tells us about her personality. What else has happened to Marlene today, you might wonder? Where is she going in the rain? *Is* someone out to get her, or is she just feeling sorry for herself?

Let's try another comparison:

1. *The arrow is trained on the target, ready to fly, but I'm waiting for just the right moment.*

2. *My ivory, curly, hip-length hair billows in the breeze and I focus my blue-green, wide eyes on the bullseye as my gloved fingers tense over my bow's string.*

Option one invites us into a tense moment, drawing us into the action that's happening and making us wonder which 'right moment' the character is waiting for. Option two, however, focuses so heavily on telling us what the main character looks like that the tension of the moment is lost between adjectives. What's wrong with this? Firstly, knowing what the character looks like doesn't give us an emotional connection with them or the story. Secondly, especially since we're in first person *and* in a high-action moment, the main character is definitely not thinking about their ivory, curly, hip-length hair. It doesn't make sense for them to describe their appearance to us in this moment.

Let's try another one:

- *Fifty-year-old Lisa was in a white, sterile hospital room when the nurse told her about the diagnosis. She began to cry, and felt sick.*

- *'I'm here for you, Mum,' said Lisa's teary daughter, gripping her hand from the chair by Lisa's hospital bed. Lisa's heart ached in response. 'People recover from this kind of disease all the time.'*

Option one gives us the facts of what's happening and tells us about the emotions. But option two draws us into emotions that are shown rather than told, inviting us into the emotional weight of a diagnosis that affects a mother and daughter's relationship. Have these examples started sparking ideas in your mind for your own first lines? If your first page relies more on context and information than action and emotion, can you play with the writing to better grasp the reader's attention?

Your book's first page will likely be 100-150 words in print. (The average word count per print page is 250, but on first pages of chapters, up to half the page is lost to the title.) These few paragraphs are the number one piece of *prime book real estate* other than the back cover description/blurb. Page one is like a billboard in Times Square compared to the rest of your book, which is closer to a tiny newspaper advertisement. People see it first when they open the book and they need to be impressed. That's why I encourage you to use your first page as *ad space* that makes readers want to buy into your work. Here, you're showing off the best of your story, the best of your writing skills, the heart of what the book is about.

As you edit, keep these thoughts in mind about what the reader really wants to read now and what can be explained later. Details can come later, once the reader is hooked. Slowly drop in information as you move through the action, and watch how this can turn a boring or generic first page into something exciting and fresh that readers will *need* to turn the page on.

Should I have a prologue?

A prologue comes before chapter one and tells readers a bit of background story that eases them into the main narrative. Now, let's bust a big myth about prologues before we even get into this section, because I will not ever let you be led astray! Notice how I said the prologue gives us background *story*? Not information. *Story.* Does that start to answer the question of whether or not to include one in your book?

This is not the place for a big exposition dump or textbook-like explanation of the characters, the world, or the history. However, in the pages before page one, some authors include visuals like maps, family trees, cast lists, glossaries, pronunciation guides, or even timelines that may include monarchies, wars, and more. These can work really well, particularly for complex sci-fi and fantasy or historical novels. Since they aren't included in the prose, the reader can choose whether or not to engage in the extra information. It's clear this isn't story, and the visuals are there as an aid, a reference point – not homework.

When a prologue is added and becomes page one, it should, naturally, function like page one. Remember, we aren't wasting our prime real estate. A prologue should be a necessary addition that adds to the story and further engages the reader. It isn't an excuse for an author to add contextual information. In all honesty, this can look lazy, because it means the author either didn't have the skill to weave context into the story, or couldn't be bothered to.

So, what makes a good prologue? It might be a flashback to an important event in the main character's past, like a childhood memory. It might be in another character's perspective, showing something relevant to the story that the protagonist may not know. For example, in a murder mystery novel, the prologue might have some clues that lead up to the crime – or even feature the crime itself from the POV of the victim or an onlooker. It isn't an exposition dump, but it also isn't another term for Chapter One – it needs to be set apart in some way, and give the reader a glimpse at something they wouldn't get from the main story.

Leigh Bardugo, author of the bestselling Grishaverse books (like *Six of Crows,* 2015), is known for her expert prologues. She takes characters who we typically never see again – sometimes they're even killed off by the end of the prologue – and gives them a scene long enough to make the reader really care for them, showing their side of life in her vividly built fantasy world. They have just enough to do with the main narrative that this mini-story impacts the plot, but overall often aren't *that important.* You could skip the prologue and still understand the story. But the key is that her prologues give us context and engage us at the same time – which is the formula for prologue perfection.

Prologues aren't necessary, and if you're unsure whether or not to include one, I'd recommend you don't. That isn't because I have anything against prologues – I used them in my *Woken Kingdom* series to show important scenes from the characters' pasts – but they need to serve a purpose. If you, as the author, aren't sure whether one is needed, the reader will probably agree.

Some readers, knowing that prologues aren't part of the *actual* story, will skip or skim over them, straight to Chapter One. I know. It's terrible. But it means the first lines of your prologue need to hook readers even better than a regular page one would. You're fighting for attention when the reader is tempted to skip those pages altogether.

If you don't know that your prologue will hook readers, you could be wasting your 'ad space'. It'd be like having a billboard and putting the product's T&Cs in a long list on it, instead of a great picture and a few words to excite potential buyers. If you haven't written a prologue, consider if one would benefit your book, and if you have, make sure it draws in the reader emotionally rather than dumping information on them.

What's exposition dumping?

Since exposition dumps (sometimes known as info-dumps) often happen at the beginning of the story, and especially often in prologues, I want to clarify what they are here, as well as why they don't work.

Exposition dumping is the term used when writers give paragraphs of information, telling the reader context in an almost textbook or essay-like format, rather than weaving explanations into the action. This is the opposite of what we were discussing above about making good first pages. Instead of drawing in the reader with *action* and *emotion*, the writer bombards them with *context*. The writer mistakenly thinks the reader needs this information to understand the story, but the block of exposition only bores the reader and takes them out of the story.

Exposition dumps often look like:

- On a larger scale:

    ○ A timeline of what's happened in the world up until now (the history of a fantasy world, for example).

    ○ An explanation of the worldbuilding, like the magic system or political landscape.

    ○ Telling the reader a character's whole life story when it isn't relevant to the story now.

- On a smaller scale:

○ A long description of a character or place's appearance, rather than weaving description into action. For a very short example: *She had brunette hair and dark eyes*, versus, *She brushed a brunette curl behind her ear and gave him a deep stare with her dark eyes.*

○ An explanation of a physical action before it happens, instead of letting the action speak for itself. For example, detailing the rules of a game before the game is played, rather than letting the reader figure out the rules *as* the game is played, or detailing the main character's job rather than simply letting us see them work.

To get back to first pages, there's no place where exposition dumping is more dangerous. This is where you have to place a strong hook and create an emotional connection with the reader. It is not the place to explain to the reader the history of the world, the current state of the world (outside what they're experiencing in the moment), the backstory of a character, the way the setting looks (in great detail), or anything else that isn't immediately exciting or emotional for the reader to devour.

How do we handle getting information across?

If the purpose of page one is to give the reader an emotional connection with the main character, then of course we need to tell the reader at least little about them. A little! So, what you *should* do is give tiny hints and tads of information, and better yet, show it, don't tell it. (See chapter 'Sentences That Engage', where we talk about 'show don't tell' in more detail.) This little piece of information must be important enough it tells us a lot, but simple enough to show in only a few words.

You might:

- Show the protagonist is witty, through a line of sarcastic dialogue.

- Show they're depressed, through the way they see the world.

- Show a quality, like their intelligence or strength, through action.

- Show a unique part of their appearance through the way they or others interact with it (like a scar).

These little nuggets help the reader make that emotional connection, be it finding the character funny, empathising with them, or being interested to know more about their background (Where did they get that scar?). But, because they're short and sweet, they engage and hook the reader, making them want to know more. Rather than pressing pause on the story to show the reader the character's entire Wiki page, we get to keep the action and excitement up.

On page one, we also want to establish the stakes. If the emotional connection with the character is the hook, then the stakes are the bait (I guess. I'm not into fishing.). Here, we're giving the reader a taste of the plot, for example:

- Is it going to be about falling in love, getting a promotion, destroying the world?

- What are we up against (what's stopping the character reaching their goal)?

- What's the worst that could happen if the main character doesn't reach their goal?

We want to hook the reader by giving them a *hint* as to what might happen in the story. Again, though, it's more important to make sure you're creating questions than answering them. Get the reader excited about what's to come! Start teasing plot points that will come up later. Just like we did with creating the emotional hook, show the stakes through action. Don't tell the reader that the world is about to end. Have the main character fret over getting enough tinned beans into their bunker.

As always, find balance. If you reveal too much or too little in the first pages, you're not making your reader excited to read on. While you want to establish what kind of person your main character is, what the stakes are, and what the book might be dealing with, you don't want to tell the reader all the secrets. Let them discover things as they go, and don't underestimate them. Readers are often smarter than you think, and don't need or want to be told everything explicitly. Allow them to fill in the gaps on their own, and keep them guessing!

The first line

If the first page of your book is your billboard, the first line is the big, showy 'SALE ON NOW' used to hook potential customers. There's nothing more important than this sentence. (Unfortunately. I know, it's a lot of pressure.) If a reader is flicking through potential reads at the bookstore, and each book's first line is an ad for the book, the reader will buy the one that stands out to them the most. This hook must make your reader immediately want to keep reading. It's all the principles we've talked about regarding your first page, but at an even more intense, vital level.

If your first line is something mundane, such as *She woke up*, or *He sat down in his chair*, or *They got in the car to go to work*, you've missed a massive opportunity to engage the reader. You get one chance to make a first impression, and this is it. If your hook is commonly used or a cliché, you're telling your reader that your work isn't going to be very creative, and that you don't have a strong narrative voice. Here are some common first line clichés so you can see what I mean:

- It was a dark, stormy night . . .

- I didn't know my life was about to change forever . . .

- Long ago . . .

- Once upon a time . . .

As you now know, what we want to do in the first page, and especially in the first line, is make that vital emotional connection to keep the reader reading. Lines that are vague or cliché aren't interesting to readers, because they've seen them a million times before. Lines that show off your author voice, your creativity, and the theme of the book, however, can do real magic. Something like, *She punched him in the face*, or *I just got fired*, is a lot more engaging than the examples above. However, it doesn't have to be so intense and action-based. Any brilliant line that teases the plot, world, or character, or that otherwise intrigues the reader, is going to be a stronger hook for your story.

Do you want to test me? Here's the first line of my debut novel, *Woken Kingdom*, in the prologue: *The princess woke with a stranger's lips on hers, his hot breath like silk on her skin.* With this line I wanted to ground the reader by showing we're in a *Sleeping Beauty* retelling, but introduce an eerie feeling so it's clear story will be twisted. Chapter one then introduces us to active and determined main character, Maya, with: *I'm tying my shoelaces, packing my bag, checking my map one more time.*

It's hard to create the perfect first line, I won't lie to you. But it's *your* novel, so I know you can sum up all the best of your work in one sentence. You've got this.

First pages in querying and editing

When an editor looks at your novel, whether they're an editor you've hired or a commissioning editor at a publishing house, they're going to look very closely at your first lines. It's their first impression of the book, and it's here that they're going to decide how much work your book might need to get it to a publishable standard.

If you're querying, at this point the commissioning editor or agent will be deciding whether or not your book is worth taking on. If their first impression isn't very good, they're going to assume the rest of the book is the same standard. Most often, since we all put so much effort into the first page, it's what editors will assume is our 'best'. If that best is a cliché or exposition dump, they're likely to send a swift rejection and move on to the next of hundreds of books from hopeful authors in their inbox.

If they have to wait a few chapters to get to the good stuff, you're already at a loss. In this day and age, you can't expect people to wait. You can't expect them to learn the entire history of your sci-fi universe before they can get into the story. This is a major red flag to agents and editors. They want to see books that are already polished, which they can make sparkle! Always present an enticing first chapter, and one last time: utilise your billboard and your hook, and show off the best you can do.

Exercise: Studying first pages

Pick a book off your bookshelf and read the first page. First, without thinking of the technical aspects, just consider how you feel about it.

Now, go through a mental checklist of what the first page does and doesn't do, based on what you learned in this chapter. Take some notes if you like. Would you say this book successfully hooks the reader, or not? Why? If you haven't read the book, consider: Are you drawn in emotionally? Do you want to turn to the next page, or is it a little plain?

If you've read the book, knowing what you do about the plot and characters, how might you rewrite the first page? Would you start in a different place entirely, or would you tweak the balance of description and action? Maybe add some emotion, or add extra context because there's so much action the reader ends up feeling lost?

With your notes in mind, are you able to go back to your novel's first page with a fresher perspective? If you were reading your book for the first time, do you think it would successfully draw you in?

13

How We Write the Story: POV, Tense, and Voice

Hey! We've finally made it past structure and we can talk about words! Let's get into the intricacies of the story and talk about the writing. That's probably what you've been most excited about, right? What we're discussing first are the overall choices we make about how we're going to write. Then, over the next few chapters, I'll be helping you learn how to complete line edits on your writing, so it really shines and feels like your own.

Voice is vital, and readers know that. For some of you, point of view (POV) and tense will come naturally. Maybe you're already pretty comfortable with this, and that's amazing. But for many newer writers, these are a big struggle, which is why I want to really nail down the concepts over this chapter. I get a lot of writers in my inbox sending me samples of their work that are full of switches between past and present tense, or cases of moving unclearly between points of view. This leaves the story very confusing to read, and I always turn away these prospective clients with a gentle, 'This isn't ready for me yet, go back and work on your craft.'

That's because my job as an editor isn't to rewrite your manuscript so it's 'correct'. Rather, it's to guide you towards improvements once you've done all you can to get it where you want it to be. If I were to spend countless hours rewriting the novel so the tense and POV are consistent, you would a) be spending far more money on your edit, and b) not be getting the high-level edit you want, because my focus would be on things you can fix yourself, instead of on what I can help you polish.

This is why developing the POV, tense, and voice aspects of your writing craft are vital before bringing in a professional editor. When an editor has to go through your work and entirely rewrite it for you because the writing is struggling with the basics, the story may not feel like your own anymore. Editors enhance your voice, but if you don't have a strong voice to enhance, there's only so much they can do. They may end up rewriting it in their own voice, or only doing basic copy edits and no higher level edits, because that's all they can really do with an undeveloped writing style. This is why I don't tend to accept manuscripts that aren't ready – I don't want to trample someone's voice when they haven't even discovered it yet.

Point of view

Point of view has a pretty literal meaning, because it's the viewpoint – both physical and emotional – that a story is told through. Also known as perspective, everyone has one (some worse than others, unfortunately). We all see life through our own eyes only, filtered through our own biases, and based on our own experiences. We almost never have the full story, and no matter how wise we think we are, it's always hard to see the bigger picture.

When we were discussing characters earlier in this book, we touched on the concept that different people have different voices; different ways of talking, moving, feeling emotions, describing things, and more. We might even see things differently physically, like viewing something from below if you're short or above if you're tall. Have you ever been back to someplace you visited as a child, and marvelled at how it felt so much bigger back then? No two writers or characters will have the exact same voice, because our viewpoint affects how we tell stories.

The point of view your book is written from, therefore, is the physical and emotional space in which you root the reader to experience the story. It's the character (body and mind) you choose to tell the story from. POV is:

- A literal, physical viewpoint, since you're telling the story from behind the character's eyes.

- A body through which to experience the five senses.

- An emotional perspective that tells the story based on the character's personality.

The only time a book isn't written from behind one or more of the characters' eyes is when the POV is *third person omniscient*, which is a somewhat outdated and unusual style in which the narrator is god-like and watches over the story. Instead of being rooted in the POV of one character, this narrator can dive into different characters' minds at any time to tell the reader what's going on from any point. This is a perfectly valid way to write, but it's difficult to pull off effectively and readers aren't always used to it, so it may be confusing. I tend to recommend authors get a closer look at their characters and keep their writing smoother by using first person or limited third.

Second person is another unusual POV. It writes as if the reader *is* the character (you/your pronouns). This can be really fun, but since it's so uncommon I'm sadly not going to go into detail on it in this book. If you want to write in second person, I recommend doing lots of research into how to do it well, and read a lot of stories in second person. It's a quite tricky and sometimes alienating POV. It's likely to take a lot of practise to get right.

Now it's time to talk about the big ones – first person and third person!

First person

- **First person** writes as if the character is telling the story *(I, we, my)*.

First person is my favourite point of view to write and read from, because I love to be deep in the character's mind, experiencing things as they experience them. A lot of books that are on the 'lighter' side of fiction, like young adult (YA) and romance novels, are written in first person. It feels fresh, modern, in the moment, and deeper in the emotions of the character.

Of course, there are drawbacks too. The main limitation of first person is that you're stuck in your POV character's head, so you can only describe the story exactly as they experience it. You don't have any wiggle room to 'zoom out' and get a bigger picture view, or to occasionally go into other characters' POVs to tell their side of the story. You also have to stick more closely to that character's voice, since they're the one telling the story, which could stifle your own style.

Here are some tips for writing and editing a book that's in first person:

- Avoid overuse of 'I', especially when beginning sentences. Aim to vary where possible, so not every sentence looks like, *I did this. I did that. I felt good.*

- Stay deep in the POV character's head, always. They can't know things they don't know, even if you really want to tell the reader. (We will talk about head hopping later.)

- Know how reliable or unreliable your narrator is, and how this impacts what the reader believes.

- Make sure their narrative voice stays consistent. (For example, you may want to write a really poetic line, but it wouldn't be in the POV character's personality to talk that way.)

What about dual POVs?

Some authors like to write in first person but still be able to go between different character's viewpoints. This is especially common in romance books, when an author wants to tell the story from two (or more) love interests' perspectives. This is a great option, but like all fun writing techniques, you have to learn to use it effectively.

When writing and editing a dual POV novel, make sure both voices are distinctive to avoid any confusion. It's common to have the POV character's name as the subtitle in the chapter (and only switch POVs between chapters). However, the reader should be able to easily tell whose viewpoint they're in whether or not they're told. If the voices blend too much, the reader could get lost or confused, unsure whose head they're in. When this happens, you need to go back and further develop the voices to ensure they're distinct. For example, by having one speak formally and the other with lots of slang.

To give you my experience, I once wrote a novel with three POVs in first person, which was a big task to handle! I never published it, and I'm not sure I'd ever do that many first person POVs again. Crafting several unique voices, and spending time in several different heads, makes for a complex story. If you can pull it off, it can be amazing. But if you're at the point of juggling a lot of first person POVs and struggling, it would be worth considering if third person might be a more effective option.

Third person

- **Third person** writes about the character, and has several of its own subcategories *(she, their, him).*

We've already touched on omniscient third person, but now I'm going to talk about the more popular third person *limited*. This is a lot like first person, in that you're in the POV character's head – you're just telling the story about them, rather than them being the one to tell the story.

Since third person can zoom in and out of the character's mind, it's a lot less restricted than first person. However, third person runs into problems when the writer struggles not to jump around viewpoints, or holds the reader at arm's length because they're staying too zoomed out and aren't delving deep into the mind of the main character.

What's zooming in and out, you ask? When you're zoomed out in third person, you're pulling back from the main character's body and mind for a little while, focusing on what's happening around them. You still can't head hop into other character's POVs, but you can get a bit of a bigger picture. Perhaps the character is watching another conversation they aren't part of, and so the story offers less of their senses and inner monologue to focus on the dialogue. When you're zoomed in (which you might call 'close third person'), you're effectively in first person except for the pronouns you use. Everything is seen directly through the character's eyes, their biases, and everything is felt through their body's experience.

This ability to zoom in and out, if balanced well, allows the book to be very well rounded, both seeing the bigger picture in appropriate moments, and being right in the POV character's emotions when it's most effective. This really helps you pack a punch, and can be a fun technique to play with.

Follow these tips when writing and editing third person:

- Be clear on who's doing what, especially when it comes to speech, when the POV character is interacting with someone who has the same pronouns. (*Terry took Larry's hand and said, 'Hey!' He squeezed his hand back, and he cried.* Not clear!)

  - However, try not to use too many names and have name-jumbly sentences. (*Larry took Terry's hand, and Terry bristled while*

Larry squeezed it.)

- Stay in the character's head by using physical descriptions, such as goosebumps from the cold, or a warming heart from love.

- When zoomed in, use character voice for flair and blend direct thoughts in with description. *Dan held up the stinking rag. Dang it. Why was this his job?* versus a more zoomed out, *Dan held up the stinking rag and swore. He wondered why he had to do this.*

Head hopping

It is so important to choose one POV or 'head' per scene and stick to it. If you switch within a scene, your reader will be pulled out of the story, left confused and jarred. This 'hopping' between 'heads' is, of course, what we call head hopping. And it's one of the things newer writers struggle with most. In trying to cover everything, to give the reader as much information as possible and build out the story, they fall into this trap of jumping around

POVs. They often do this by accident, or don't realise it's a problem, but it makes the book very difficult to read.

Let me give you an example:

George walked to the grocery store and thought over the things he needed to buy for nachos tonight. Corn chips, beans, cheese . . . The automatic doors swung open, and a staff member greeted him with a smile. The greeter was thinking about how badly they wanted to get home and have their own dinner. George smiled back but bristled from cold as he went to the fridges to find his favourite cheese.

Here, we see two characters' thoughts in the same paragraph. It feels jarring, and you might be able to imaging how in first person, it might be even more confusing. Even in third person, from George's thoughts we know we're in his head in this scene – and if we're in his head, we can't possibly know what the staff member is thinking. Jumping around like this affects the natural flow of narration. It pulls the reader out of the story and impacts their reading experience. (The only time it would be okay to have a paragraph like this is if you were in omniscient third person. Even then, I would recommend keeping different people's thoughts to different paragraphs and keep hopping minimal, to help with clarity and ease the sense of whiplash.)

Head hopping encompasses more than direct thoughts. It also happens when you mention something the POV character couldn't know about another character, or know for certain. This is most often in reference to emotions. Let's say you as the writer know a non-POV character is upset. You can *show* their sadness, or have the POV character guess or assume they're sad, but you can't tell the reader with certainty. The POV isn't in their body, so we can't feel their emotions. Sometimes this means we have to add what look like redundancies (which we'll discuss more later in this book) to clarify. If the POV character's narration is, *Henry is really tired,* but they don't *know* this, *Henry must be really tired*, can be better. Better yet, you could show rather than tell: *Henry rubs his eyes and yawns.*

In first person, head hopping is an absolute no, always, under any circumstance. Okay, unless the POV character is a mind reader or something. But if you've picked a POV to stick with, now you're stuck there. You can't move outside their observations, unless you're writing in dual

POV – and even then, you can only have one POV per scene.

In third person, head hopping is a bit more compli- cated, because although we're rooted in one POV, re- alistically you can jump to anyone's POV at any time if you want to – as long as there's a scene or chapter break. A lot of writers get caught up here. I see this in a lot of books I edit, and even in some published books. Writers get confused about when, where, and how to talk about other characters' thoughts and feel- ings. This might be because they've read third person omniscient books and not realised limited third person has different rules. It's okay if that's you – writing can be confusing and it takes time to learn these things.

To clarify, you can only change POVs in third person when:

- You're in an omniscient POV that can 'dive into' different heads and see the bigger picture.

- You start a new section/scene (with a line break).

- You start a new chapter.

Otherwise, you have to write from one mind and body. This can be a bit of pressure, because it means you have to strategise to make sure you're in the best POV. Does the character you've chosen have a strong emotional connection to the scene? Does their level of understanding of what's happening around them best impact the narration? Does their POV help the reader understand the scene, or are they too limited? Conversely, do they know too much, or are they feeling too much, to effectively narrate the scene?

If you find you keep accidentally moving into other POVs in a scene, chapter, or even throughout the book, consider whether you've chosen the right main character. Often in the editing stage, as writers read back their work, it'll be a side character that calls to them more. They realise another character is more suited to being the main POV, and making this change is a big overhaul but often a fruitful one.

Here are some ways you might move out of head hopping and get across information more smoothly:

- When the POV character tells the reader about another character's thoughts and emotions, have them make an assumption instead, or show the other character's body language.

- If the reader needs to learn information the POV character doesn't or can't know, have the POV character happen upon the information, for example by overhearing a conversation.

- Make the POV character just a little unreliable in the way they tell the story. Their emotions or biases can make them miss something that's right in front of them, but the reader may be able to put the pieces together. For example, it might be very obvious that the love interest likes them, but the POV character is too insecure to believe it.

When editing your work, keep the reader in mind at all times and remember that you aren't simply telling them a story. You want them to *experience* the story, and this means ensuring they have a level of comfort and ease when reading. Cutting out head hopping can be difficult, especially if you're used to relying on it, but it will immediately benefit the story. Remember that this is a very common issue. It can be solved, though, and I believe in you!

Tense

Is your book written in past, present, or future tense? This is another one a lot of new authors struggle with, but getting your tenses right is vital. Otherwise, the writing becomes incredibly confusing to the reader. Just like with your POV, you've got to pick one tense and stick to it – so make sure it's the one you're most comfortable with for the novel you're writing.

What are the tenses in fiction?

- **Past:** The story has already happened, and is being told from a future point in time (*was, had*).

  - Because most readers are used to past tense (it's most common), it can feel 'invisible'. They don't think about it, so they more easily get lost in the story.

- **Present:** The story is happening as it's being told (*is, has*).

  - Present keeps readers right in the action and emotion as it's currently happening. It can be gripping and incredibly effective, but in general it's not as 'invisible'.

- **Future:** The story is going to happen (*will, will have*).

  ○ Unusual and tricky to do effectively.

There's no right or wrong option, but there are more popular tenses in different genres. Past is often used in epic fantasy novels, historical fiction, mystery, children's fiction, and classics. Present is often used in YA, romance, contemporary, literary, or other 'lighter' genres (since it can feel more straightforward and fresh). When it comes to choosing the tense for your book, don't feel boxed in based on what's most common. Readers are used to different tenses being used, so you get to choose what works best for you and for your story.

As you edit your novel for tense, you want to make sure your verbs always agree. Like any inconsistencies in fiction, readers pick up on errors in tense and it pulls them out of the story. A book without correct tense won't be taken seriously by agents and traditional publishers. It may even be rejected by editors you want to hire because it needs more work before professional editing. If you're serious about writing but struggle with tense, it's really important to learn how to get it right.

Here are some examples to give you an idea of verb agreement:

- Wrong: *I **give** this book a 5 star review **yesterday**.*

- Right: *I **gave** this book a 5 star review **yesterday**.*

- Wrong: *Our cafe **offers** food that **tasted** good.*

- Right: *Our cafe **offers** food that **tastes** good.*

There are a lot of ways to play with tense. It's actually pretty exciting! One sentence can be written so many ways depending on the tense you choose and the flow or meaning you want. For example:

- *She was writing.*

- *She wrote.*

- *She has written.*

- *She has been writing.*

- *She is writing.*

- *She will be writing.*

- *She will write.*

These don't all mean the same thing, and they'll fit into different scenes or sentence structures with varying effectiveness. If you were to read each of the above aloud, what might you garner from each one? It becomes clear quickly that it's more than just picking anything and rolling with it. Tense can often change an entire sentence, more than simply the verbs, because different tenses work better with different word choices and sentence structures. That's why editing for tense is more than just changing a 'was' to an 'is' – it's looking at the flow of each sentence. When editing, if you find a verb that doesn't match, don't just correct the tense and move on. Read through the whole sentence and make sure the flow is still there, like I've done here:

- Wrong: *Laurence knew the grass* **needs to be cut,** *so he got the lawnmower out to do it tomorrow.*

- Right: *Laurence knew the grass* **needed to be cut,** *so he got the lawnmower out to do it tomorrow.*

- Right: *Laurence knew the grass* **needed cutting**, *so he got the lawnmower out to do it tomorrow.*

I think the second 'right' option flows more smoothly. It also removes redundant words, which is a plus. Changing the tense became an edit to improve flow as well as verb agreement. However, you might think the first right option is best, and hey – that's the beauty of writing! Learning to play with tense is more than just getting it right. It's about learning this aspect of your author voice.

When can you change tense?

There are, of course, times when changing up the tense is fine, or even expected. Most often, you'll see this in flashbacks. Even if a book is written in present tense, the flashback will appear in past tense to show it happened in the past. Also, some writers will use different tenses for different POVs to help differentiate dual POV or dual timeline books.

When writing in past tense, sometimes you'll describe something that's true at present as well. In this case, it might be suitable to use present tense. For example, '*Sandra **walked** through the tech store. She really **wanted** a new phone, but they **are** so expensive. She **walked** right back out again.*' Personally, I find this clunky and confusing, but many authors do it and it isn't technically seen as wrong.

Past within past

What about when you're writing in past tense, but telling the story of something that happened before the book's 'now'?

Okay, this sounds complicated, but I promise it isn't too hard. Your 'now' is the timeline the story is being told in. Even if you're in past tense, you're still showing a moment unfolding. But let's say you skip from Friday to Monday in the 'now', then have the character explain what happened to them on Saturday. In this *past*-past tense, you can use 'had' to ground the reader in the timeline, clarifying what's happening 'now' and what's already unfolded.

These definitions can help us make the distinction:

- **Past simple** (it happened in the book's 'now'): *She raced to the top of the hill.*

- **Past perfect** (it happened before the book's 'now'): *She* had *raced to the top of the hill.*

With those definitions in mind, I created the following example using three different types of past tense: *Nina plonked down the shopping bags in her living room and sighed. She had already put up the Christmas tree, a task that took her hours, but when John had come over, he'd called it tacky. She was going to take it down ASAP.*

The first sentence is in the 'now' with 'plonked' and 'sighed'. The second details a previous event with 'had already', 'had come', and 'he'd'. The third details something that she plans to do in the future, with 'was going to'. Although we're talking about different times, it's very clear to the reader what's happening now, previously, and in the future. When editing past perfect, just be careful not to use 'had' too much, because it can become redundant and clunky. Contractions can help with this, like shortening 'she had' to 'she'd'.

Putting POV and tense together

Many writers have a preferred POV and tense to write in that resonates with them the most. It might come naturally, without them even consciously thinking of the rules. But, sometimes we realise there's a way to write a book that just makes more sense with the narrative. A fast-paced thriller might call for first-person present tense, even if you're more used to third-person past tense. Remember that any choice can work well – it's up to you to make it sparkle.

Let's look at how different tenses and POVs work together:

- First/Present: *I drink from the glass, needing the hydration.*

- First/Past: *I drank from the glass; I needed the hydration.*

- Third/Present: *She drinks from the glass, needing the hydration.*

- Third/Past: *She drank from the glass; she needed the hydration.*

If you're editing your novel and keep running into cases of the narration feeling off, but you're not sure why, look at your POV and tense. Evaluate whether you're using the most natural and effective option for your story. Overhauling to a new POV or tense is a big job, but it can be more than worth the trouble if it gets your story to where it needs to be. Try reading your work out loud when written in different POV/tense blends – which reads most comfortably?

Exercise: Transform POV and tense in a scene

For this exercise, pick a scene from your novel or a scene from any novel of your choosing that you'd like to have a go at transforming. We're going to play with the POV and tense to see how they can impact the way a scene is told, the way it feels, and the level of information the reader is allowed to know.

Read through your chosen scene and identify whose POV the scene is told from, and what tense it's written in. I'm not going to tell you exactly what to do here. You might want to go from first person to third person, or go even further and try second, omniscient third, or even jump into another character's head and tell the scene from their POV instead.

You might even stay in the same character's viewpoint but imagine them as a very different person. If your protagonist was a bully instead of a pacifist, for example, how would their narration change? We're about to talk more about voice, but I want you to start identifying on your own how the tone changes as you move through different narration options.

You can try just one transformation, or challenge yourself to do a few versions. This can help you really get a feel for what's most natural to you, and what works best for the scene. Of course, in a novel, you can't change the tense or POV whenever you feel like it just to suit the scene, but does this exercise make you wonder if a different POV or tense would suit the overall book better?

This exercise helps with the editing stage because it starts to allow you to identify what's working and what isn't in your prose. When we try something entirely new with a scene, it helps us break out of how close we are to it and see it from a different perspective, which can be great in helping us to improve our storytelling.

Voice

Beyond POV and tense, which are more technical aspects of writing, developing your novel's narrative voice is where you get to be really creative. Is your book going to be witty or serious? Is it a gritty crime novel, a flowery period drama, or a light-hearted, silly kid's book? How do you normally tell stories, and how do you want readers to feel as they read your prose?

Remember, there are two voices at play here: your POV character's, and your own. Pulling the two together is what makes a book feel unique, crafted expertly in your tone while diving deep into a character who may be nothing like you. Your voice should also keep in mind your genre and audience, and what kind of tone will resonate with those readers. And, of course, what's natural to you as a writer!

Everyone thinks differently, and that's what we draw on most when crafting voice. Consider how a typical child would describe something compared to how a typical elderly person would. Or how someone poor might see something compared to someone rich. To the poor child, everything is big and new. To the rich older person, everyday occurrences may lack novelty. Therefore, in fiction, we use these concepts, understanding the character's background and personality, to create an authentic voice.

We all talk so differently, from the words we use and our sentence structure, to the way we describe things and the way we tell a story. A generic narrative voice makes a novel lose atmosphere, characterisation, and impact. Great voices, however, make stories highly engaging. They make the reader feel as if they're right there with the characters. For example, even though *this* book is largely informative and certainly isn't fiction, there's plenty of my voice in here – especially since I'm writing in first person. I like to speak right to you! It makes reading more interesting than if I'd written this like a textbook, right?

It can be difficult though, in fiction, when your own voice as a writer shines through too much and overshadows the POV character. Learning to balance both – allowing your unique writing style to glow through your work while also giving your main character a strong voice that doesn't just sound like you – is a skill we gain through studying other authors' work and practicing putting ourselves in our characters' shoes.

Dialects, accents, and slang are also great for characterisation and placing a character/story in a specific setting. This might help to show the country and area you're in, but might also be part of worldbuilding in SFF settings. Some authors create entire languages for their novels. (If you're going to use slang or languages other than English, the trick is to make sure the reader can still understand what's going on and pick up on what things mean based on context. If not, they'll be totally lost!)

How do you find and cultivate your story's narrative voice and tone? Here are some ways to play and practise:

- Try to write from the POV of different characters in your novel. How might the villain tell the same story as the hero?

- Physically act out and read aloud scenes as if you're the character narrating the story. Does it feel natural? If it's first person, does it feel as if they're talking to the reader, or does it feel flat?

- Consider how the character's worldview effects the way they see things. How does their personality impact what they say? You can give them any topic and write a monologue to practise weaving their opinions and beliefs into the prose.

Unreliable narration

Can you trust the voice that's telling the story? Unreliable narration, particularly through first person, is a great way to have your character mislead the reader and show their 'voice'. Maybe there's something they know about a crime that is only revealed at the end, or maybe you see the story from two perspectives, and they differ enough you know one is deceitful.

This adds so much colour to a story, and it doesn't have to be ominous. Unreliable narration could be as simple as writing from the perspective of a very unobservant character who often misses things. Alternatively, you could have a character who overthinks everything, causing them to jump to incorrect conclusions.

Unreliable narration is always fun to write, but make sure you have the skill to do it well, or you may just end up annoying your readers by not delivering on your promises. The reader should be able to sense when something is off – if everything comes as a big surprise in a plot twist they couldn't have seen coming, the unreliable narration didn't do its job. That's because, once again, we always want the story to feel realistic. Balance giving the reader enough hints to know something isn't right and not giving them all the secrets.

Editing voice

Remember that sometimes 'errors' can enhance voice – like using clunky writing to show a character's confusion – so be cautious of what you edit and how. A huge reason I caution against spellcheckers is that they tend to not understand the nuances of storytelling. They can ruin a great line because they want everything to sound uniform and 'correct'.

These are some better ways authors can improve their voice when editing:

- Find sentences or descriptions that are generic or cliché and reword them to be more unique and realistic to the POV character.

- Dictate (Speech-to-Text) to retell a scene you've

written. When the dictation adds punctuation, notice how the flow changes. It can be interesting to see how differently we speak out loud compared to how we write.

- Look for instances of your character's voice feeling inconsistent or 'out of character'. Sometimes it's normal to act a bit different to usual, for example if you're upset and acting out, but outside of these scenarios, characters should remain consistent.

- If you have more than one POV, open to a random page in your writing where you can't see who's POV you're in (for example with a subheading), and see if you're able to guess. This can help you ensure each character has a distinct narrative voice that makes the POV clear.

Exercise: Talk like someone else

Have you ever tried writing a story in a voice that's nothing like your own? For this exercise, I'd like you to step into someone else's shoes and write a short journal entry from their point of view. Better yet, take a real-life event that happened to you recently and retell it through a different lens.

You might usually write in a tone that's very natural for you, not thinking much about the biases that dictate how you see the world. Now, I want you to try the exact opposite! How would a person who is completely different to you speak, based on their life experience and personality? Are they more laid back or highly strung? Are they very posh or very casual? As you write your journal entry, try to fully immerse yourself and be that character. Don't go back and edit – just have fun and write as you go, not worrying about the story at all but the voice. There doesn't really have to be any plot.

When you're done (and you can go as long as you feel like!), go back and pay attention to the ways you made your voice sound different to your usual style. Did you use different word choices, put commas in unusual places, use more or fewer contractions? Maybe your sentences were shorter or longer than usual, or you used lots of description where you normally wouldn't pay that much attention to your surroundings.

How did you feel about this exercise? Looking back at your book draft, do you feel you balanced your voice and your POV character's voice well?

14

The Building Blocks of Fiction Prose

We're making our way down the editing funnel. Are you enjoying learning all about editing the sentence level of a book? We still have a while to go, but don't worry. I'm right here with you. Since we're getting into narrower concepts now, try not to overwhelm yourself with too much information at once. Try to take breaks, and re-read chapters as you go to help you better retain everything you're learning. Remember this book is always here for you as a guide – you don't have to do everything at once, and you don't have to keep it all in your head. Use this book to make your work easier, not harder.

In this chapter, we're doing a quick dive into the four main aspects of writing that we can break a fiction story's prose into. I want to familiarise you with the purpose of sentences before we get deeper into how we craft each line. These are the building blocks I'll be talking about:

- **Description:** How the senses play in the novel, from appearances and smells to emotions and feelings.

- **Action:** The physical movement occurring in the novel.

- **Dialogue:** The words characters say aloud; the conversations they have with each other.

- **Inner Monologue:** The POV character's thoughts, whether it's a quick line or a long monologue on their feelings.

When we edit, we want to make sure all four elements are in balance and harmony (and that the *Fire Nation* doesn't attack) throughout the novel. Relying too heavily on one or two can become not only tiring to the reader, but also mean you're lacking depth in certain areas. For example, a book that's heavy on description will be very atmospheric, but if the reliance on description means less inner monologue, the reader may not feel connected to the main character.

The hardest part of editing our prose elements is identifying the imbalances. Then it's simply a matter of finding ways to round out the narration. When you read back over a scene you've written, simply look deeply at which element each sentence and paragraph serves. Many writers will even go in with a highlighter (on your computer or on a printed out manuscript), colour coding each sentence with an element. When they lean back and look at how much each colour shows up, they often find imbalances where they never would have picked up on them. It can be shocking, but the fix is simple: once you identify a significant imbalance, you can edit to shorten prose where one element is taking over, or add an element where it doesn't show up enough.

You'll also find that adjusting the balance works well in different scenes that serve different purposes. In a high-stakes fight scene, you'll of course see a lot of action, with less visual description and inner monologue. This is because the character is so focused on what's happening in the moment that they don't have time to narrate about what the setting looks like, or have a long introspective moment. However, after the fight, they might have a lot of inner monologue as they go over what happened, a moment low on action as they sit and contemplate.

Here's an example of using all four elements in just one paragraph: *Dana slams her hand down on the table.* (Action.) *'What do you mean?'* (Dialogue.) *Her fingers turn red, matching the tomatoes on her dinner plate.* (Description.) *She can't believe how dense her family can be.* (Inner monologue.)

Of course, you don't need to use all four in just one paragraph, but I want you to notice how using a good balance creates colour, flow, and engagement. Often you will have a few paragraphs at a time with just one element, and this can be just as effective. You might draw out a long, poetic description to bring the reader into a setting, or have a page that's only dialogue with a few action beats, which draws the reader into a heated argument.

As you edit your work, keep an eye on your use of each element. You'll likely be drawn to one or two and naturally use them more, while others are harder for you. That's entirely okay, and the balance doesn't have to be exact –

remember, your voice and the way you want to tell the story is important too. But keep practising the ones you struggle with and study how other authors balance theirs. You never know what you'll discover.

Exercise: Finding balance

Pick a scene in your book or another book, and identify which writing element is used most. For this exercise, I want you to play with the balance and rewrite the scene in different ways to see how it comes across when you prioritise one element over the others.

Let's say there's a fight scene that's heavy on action. It wouldn't be the appropriate place to have a lot of inner monologue, but what if you rewrote the scene so there *was*? What would change with all this added introspection, and how would you adjust how you tell the story so it still feels effective?

What about description? If you took a scene and added a line of description to every single paragraph, what might happen? Does it become jolty and strange, or does it actually bring more atmosphere?

As you play with the elements, make sure to keep an eye on your writing. Remember, this exercise is to help you learn, and that means having a good look at which elements you might be over or under utilising, as well as how you use them. How does your writing change as you flow through the elements? Which do you rely on most, and which do you find comes most naturally to you? Do one or more need a little work? It's all about identifying weak areas so you can practise your craft and continue improving as a writer.

15

Sentences That Engage

We're now at an even deeper level of line editing (yay!) and that's making each sentence sing! Whether it's description, dialogue, action, or inner monologue, as we discussed in the last chapter, each sentence can be structured and reworked to be more flowy, effective, and engaging. In this chapter, we're going to talk about sentence length, passive versus active voice, and showing instead of telling.

Sentence length and rhythm

There's no right or wrong sentence length.

But we can absolutely use varying sentence lengths to make scenes flow better. In general, less is more. Long sentences can be the perfect addition to your writing, but with too many they can bore your readers, cause them to skip ahead, zone out, or lose interest completely and stop reading. This is why some classic novels can feel almost painful to read, even if we're loving the story. Short sentences tend to be easier because the reader gets through them faster.

If a lot of your sentences are longer than about twenty-five words, see which can be split in half or reworded. Don't think I'm against long sentences, though. When used sparingly, they can draw the reader in for winding prose that brings them right in and doesn't let them stop for a breath. This can feel especially poetic or romantic, making long sentences great for scene setting or describing emotions. The trick is to not have too many and risk losing the reader's short attention span.

Meanwhile, short sentences are fantastic for high-tension, high-speed scenes. They create a fast flow that readers speed through, which gives the effect of things happening quickly. If a sentence is less than four to six words, just make sure it's a full sentence – most of the time. Sometimes, using non-full sentences, though not 'correct', can create a staccato effect. (*Did. She. Really. Just. Do. That?*) This can be a great addition, showing disbelief or shock. Always remember the importance of voice, and that you can and should play with extra-long and extra-short sentences when it helps enhance a scene.

Of course, we then have medium-length sentences, which will make up the majority of your book. To vary them, look at where you can move around commas and where different words could go. When you're editing your work, read for a sense of rhythm and try to consistently change it up. Reading your work aloud can be great for this. You'll quickly realise where the sentences are feeling too repetitive, or don't quite match the kind of impact you're going for. If the rhythm starts to tire, with too many sentences that sound the same, rework the sentence structure so it keeps the reader more engaged.

Gingerly, Portia picked up the cat, trying to scratch it behind the ears. Unfortunately, the cat didn't like that, and it bit her. However, she kept the cat held in the air, until it calmed down. If she was lucky, it would come home with her, and she'd have a new pet.

Notice in the above example how all the sentences are written with the same length and rhythm? I find it very fatiguing, even though it's only a short paragraph! Let's try something different:

Portia gingerly picked up the cat and scratched it behind the ears. Unfortunately, the cat didn't like that. It bit her! She still kept the cat held in the air, waiting for it to calm down. If she was lucky, it would come home with her, and she'd have a new pet.

I really didn't change much in this second option. It's the same story. But by shuffling around some words and punctuation, varying the length and rhythm, I created a paragraph that's a lot more engaging to read. As you edit your own book, keep an eye on your sentence length and rhythm. Try to change things up and see which combinations you like best.

Show don't tell

For so many authors, 'show don't tell' is hard to understand and even harder to implement. And I'm sorry to say this, because despite it being a tough one, it is absolutely so worth it. I know this from my own experience – this is one of the pieces of writing advice that took me forever to get, but now I can do it, my writing is far better than before. Because I've struggled with it myself, I'm going to use this chapter to explain the concept as best I can and hold your hand through it. Hopefully, then, you can move forward and improve your writing skills with ease.

Even though we hear 'show don't tell' over and over again, many authors struggle to grasp what, exactly, it means. Even if you understand the definition, you might still struggle to figure out how to actually do it in a story. And do it *effectively*. Why, then, is this difficult 'rule' so important? Showing can be used across all four of the writing elements we talked about earlier, but it's best used for description, and is particularly amazing at improving how we write about emotions. Showing fully drops the reader into the character's body and the scene unfolding around them. It makes the reader feel like they're really *there* rather than simply being told a story. Showing is like magic for a novel. It makes everything shimmer.

When we tell, we say exactly what's happening, usually in one or two words, and expect the reader to visualise and believe it. (*I was devastated.*) Showing, however, gives the reader visualisation and proof. It allows them to draw their own conclusions based off context, immersing them in the story. (*I fell to my knees, my heart aching like it never had before. I was in pieces, and I didn't know if I'd ever be able to put myself back together.*)

Telling is easier, and it's what we might be more used to. In natural speech, for example, we're not likely to tell our friends how the line at the bank was so long it made our chests ache with impatience, how we tapped our feet and kept glancing at the clock. We'll just tell them we were irritated and impatient because it took forever to get our cash out. They'll get that. But how often does someone tell you a story so wild that you wonder if it's all completely true? It seems they must have exaggerated or misremembered parts. You just cannot believe it happened, and even though they're adamant it did. Surely they only *think* they saw aliens in the night sky, and they're wrong!

This is why, in novels, showing is so important. We *can* suspend our disbelief and believe they really saw aliens, but it's easier with 'proof'. Strong showing that grounds us in the experience makes the story feel real. It doesn't let the reader go, doesn't let them back off to think about how ridiculous it is that aliens are invading – because they're too immersed in the story to wonder.

To help you understand the difference, here are some more examples of telling versus showing:

- **Told**: *John was absolutely delighted.*

- **Shown**: *John grinned widely, clapping his hands.*

- **Told**: *The forest is beautifully lush.*

- **Shown**: *The trees are dense and verdant, with shrubs around our feet and moss softening each footstep.*

- **Told**: *The wine tasted great.*

- **Shown**: *The wine was smooth on my tongue, its perfumed, fruity taste sending ripples of pleasure through me as I sipped.*

Showing also helps us have the characters interact with their scenery in a more engaging way. Rather than telling us their dress is made of silk, show us how the material feels against their skin. Rather than mentioning the beach has soft sand, show us how the characters struggle to trudge through it. Don't tell me it's a sunny day, but show me the character shielding their eyes. This connects the setting and characters, and makes for a more realistic story.

Remember head hopping? Showing helps us with this too. As we touched on earlier, the POV character may not be able to know for sure that their best friend is feeling an emotion like anger, but by showing the reader their red face and clenched fists, they can understand this through the descriptive proof. We can even show the reader things that the POV character might not pick up on, for example another character acting suspicious – eyes darting around, sweat on their brow – showing the reader they're lying about something. The reader can tell something shifty is going on, even if the MC doesn't notice, *or* maybe doesn't want to notice.

Please don't think everything has to be shown and that telling is always bad. There's a time and place for both. In fact, a book written only in show would be a bit boring, because you'd be leaning on so much description, with so many words added, that it could make the book drag out all the way to Yawnville. Telling can be great, particularly in fast-paced scenes where you don't have time for much description, or when the thing you're describing isn't of huge importance – sometimes you just have to say what you want to say, and move on!

When editing your book for the 'show don't tell' rule, evaluate how many sentences show and how many tell. Try colour-coding each line if that helps you. Is there too much telling, leaving the book lacking depth and immersion? Or is there too much showing, making the book a bit sloggy and slow, particularly in scenes that need to feel fast? Play with both in your scenes to find what works best, and if you're not sure because you're too deep in your own work to see what's working or not, ask a friend their thoughts.

Active versus passive voice

Like showing and telling, the balancing of active and passive sentences is often a problem amongst amateur writers. In the same way that people seem naturally drawn to telling, they also seem to go for passive writing before active writing. And, just like 'show don't tell', the rule of keeping sentences active is one that many writers struggle to figure out. (I did too, so don't worry, you're not alone.)

First – passive sentences are not wrong. Just like telling, they have their purpose, and sprinkling them in helps with the rhythm of your writing (like when we talked about varying sentence length). However, too much passive and your book quickly starts to feel like it's taking two steps forward and one step back. It's exhausting and slow.

What's the difference between an active sentence and a passive sentence?

- **Active sentences:** Direct, usually less in word count, and more engaging. Active voice is when the subject (character, object, etc.) performs the action of the verb (doing word). *She jumped up in the air.*

- **Passive sentences:** Indirect, longer, unnecessarily complex. They can distance the reader from the character/story. Passive voice is when the verb (doing word) takes precedence over the subject (character, object, etc.). *The air was jumped into* *by the woman.*

Since active and passive voice are mostly concerned with subject and verb use, they're most often concerned with the 'action' element of story writing. Often, you can spot a passive sentence with words like 'by', 'were', 'was' or even 'because'. Here are some more examples:

- **Passive:** *Because the gate was locked, they took a different path.*

- **Active:** *They took a different path because the gate was locked.*

- **Passive:** *The car was where I walked to.*

- **Active:** *I walked to the car.*

- **Passive:** *The dog was fed by its owner.*

- **Active:** *The owner fed the dog.*

- **Passive:** *The book was written by the writer.*

- **Active:** *The writer wrote the book.*

Notice how the active sentences are more engaging and faster to read? I would say at least 80% of your book should be written in active voice. Passive can then be used strategically to add some rhythm to your sentences in scenes where it has the ideal impact. For example, if the main character is experiencing a traumatic event and is dissociated from their body, passive voice can show how they're feeling as if things are happening to them, but they aren't fully present. It moves us away from the action and characters.

Check for active and passive sentences when editing your own work. Where can you make your writing more exciting with active sentences? Or, where can you slow down the pace or change the rhythm with a passive sentence?

Exercise: Rewriting

To help you practise varying sentence length, and using showing and active voice, for this exercise I don't want you to work on your book but to pick one off your shelf. Open to a random page, and read through it. Identify first which elements are being used, and then look at the sentences and their lengths, plus whether they're in show or tell, and active or passive. You may want to type up the page on your computer so you can do some highlighting or formatting to make this really clear.

Next, start rewriting! You can write the scene in your own voice or try to retain the author's even as you change the sentences (as an editor would do). The main idea is to say the same thing, but in different ways. Don't change the story, but try out different combinations of sentence structure. You might:

- Only use short, medium, or long sentences.

- Only write in show or only write in tell.

- Only write in passive or only in active.

- Write in long, passive sentences.

- Write in tell, with short, active sentences.

- Use a mix of all options, seeing which sentences work best in different ways.

16

The Words We Use

Well done, dear author! We have finally made it into the copy editing level of your work – the editing that people are most familiar with, and often believe is all editing is! Here, we're concerned with the words you use, the grammar and punctuation you use, and how all this fits into a fiction novel. Over the next few chapters, we'll talk about grammar, but let's start with the words we're using. I want you to have all the right definitions before moving forward.

This means talking about word classes, because you may hear words like 'noun' or 'adverb' a lot, but not really know what those mean. I always struggled to remember word classes, especially when they tried to teach me them at school. I've always been more of an intuitive writer, so all these funny rules often do my head in for a long time before they click. What I really needed was to have a good explanation of what the word classes mean, and why it's important to understand them – *and* why they give us a bit of a cheat code to stronger writing!

Nouns

A noun is simply the name of something. In fiction, this includes your characters and places, but more broadly can refer to any object. Almost every sentence will have a noun (or pronoun or proper noun), because the sentence has to be about *something*. For example: *person, arm, country, pen, chair, flower, hot chippie, etc* . . . It's how other words are used around the noun that creates meaning.

Proper nouns are the official/given name of something (*Emma, Hyundai*) and always need a capital letter. **Common nouns**, like 'park' or 'cat', however, don't need a capital. For example, you might call me a woman, writer, or author, but my given name is Poppy! Sometimes writers get confused about whether to capitalise titles, like 'sir' or 'queen'. Some writers deviate as part of their style sheet, but in general you use capitals only when it's a title that's part of a proper noun. For example, 'She's the queen,' but 'There's a statue of Queen Anna.'

Pronouns

A pronoun is used in place of a noun when, rather than using a name, you use words like *it, she, they,* or *you.* In fiction, knowing when to use pronouns helps make your book engaging and understandable. For example, when writing dialogue between two people with different pronouns, it's great to use pronouns such as 'he said' and 'she said' for a while, after first establishing who the speakers are. This feels a lot cleaner than using their names over and over. Names can feel clunky! With more speakers, however, or speakers with the same pronouns, it's important to use names where there may be confusion.

Adjectives

Adjectives are descriptive attributes that pair with nouns. They could be the colour of something, the shape and size, or even an opinion (*it sucks!*). We use them in description to clarify and bring atmosphere. *The **old** chair was **rotten**, and needed a **keen-eyed** expert to refurbish it to its **original** state.*

Be careful not to overuse adjectives in your description. Always consider if there are more concise ways to describe things. Instead of, *The small, baby cat purred,* just say, *The kitten purred.*

Verbs

Verbs describe action – anything from 'loves' to 'occurred'. This means verbs are the words we use that show tense. Mastering the use of verbs allows you to show readers whether you're talking about the past, present, or future. Using this sentence as an example, 'ran' and 'arrived' are the verbs: *She **ran** to the party, but **arrived** on time.* I'll refer you back to when we talked about tense for more on getting this right.

Adverbs

Adverbs give us more information about an action, similarly to how an adjective gives more information about a person or object. They typically tell you more about how the action of the verb was performed. *She **carefully** picked the flower, **almost** breaking it.* Usually adverbs end with *-ly,* and we'll talk about why they're often redundant in the next chapter.

Prepositions

Prepositions can connect nouns to their sentence, and are most often written before the noun to show location. Common examples are *in, to, of,* and *on. They headed **toward** the beach and crossed **over** the sand.* Like adverbs, prepositions may be redundant so it's important to keep them minimal.

Conjunctions

Conjunctions connect words together to form sentences. *But, because, so.* In fiction, you can be more playful with conjunctions and their use in sentence structure. For example, you can occasionally use an incomplete sentence to show the voice of your character or narrator. *I didn't want to hear that.* **But** *I think I needed to*, reads differently to, *I didn't want to hear that*, **but** *I think I needed to.*

And, you can absolutely start sentences with conjunctions. Despite the rumours, there's no existing rule that says this isn't allowed in English. We're taught not to do this because it feels informal. Starting with words like 'so' or 'and' can create shorter, snappier sentences. They feel more realistic because the casual tone often fits our characters' voices more.

Interjections

Interjections are abrupt remarks or exclamations, typically used in dialogue to express emotion or personality. *No! I had no idea.* These are especially fun to use in fiction, to create realistic and sometimes funny dialogue. Interrupting can be a fun tool to use, especially when it's to increase the sense of urgency, or create shock.

17

Bad Words

No, I don't care how many F-bombs you drop in your novel, but it has to be said that not all words are created equal – especially when it comes to fiction writing and editing. There are bad, bad words we want to avoid.

Remember that in books, each page, each line, and each word represents sought-after real estate. In other words, you're up against your reader's attention span, and your potential for profits, considering that each extra page will cost a bit extra to print, making you or your publisher less per sale. Yes, this is something publishers seriously take into consideration, which is why it's so hard to get a debut novel traditionally published if it's over industry standard word count.

You don't want extra words anywhere you don't absolutely want them to be. And no – I have nothing against long books. They just shouldn't be long for no good reason. An overuse of filler words, tentative words, adverbs, repetition, and overwriting creates a story that's far longer than it needs to be, far less effective in its storytelling, and overall lacking in engagement. Readers are left frustrated and may put the book down.

Start by reading through your manuscript carefully. If you were to omit a word, sentence, or paragraph, how might it impact the reader's understanding of the story? If the impact is low, you may want to consider rewriting or omitting it.

Here's an example:

Carrie shivered as she took in the looming grey walls of the university that she was about to step into for the first time.

'Are you coming or not?' urged her friend Lila, stepping side to side. Lila was impatient.

Carrie, however, was more concerned with the magnitude of the moment. 'This is the start of our lives. Let me take it in.'

What would you cut here? You might have noticed that *Lila was impatient* isn't necessary, since we see her impatience through her dialogue and action. It's telling when showing is already doing the work. Similarly, *Carrie, however, was more concerned with the magnitude of the moment* is unnecessary when we already know she's ruminating on the present. This sentence holds a little more weight, drilling in the idea that Carrie is feeling a sense of importance, but it still could be reworked or omitted.

Let's look at a different example:

Marcus's chihuahua yapped at his feet. The dog was small, with a rounded head and large eyes. It wanted food, and, gazing at the creature's big brown eyes and fluffy white body, Marcus found it hard to resist giving the dog another treat.

Here, we can easily take out, *The dog was small, with a rounded head and large eyes.* We already know what a chihuahua looks like (unless this was a children's novel where the target audience may not have such a broad general knowledge), so this information tells us nothing. However, the next line, with the '*big brown eyes*' and '*fluffy white body*' tells us how this chihuahua differs from others, and helps us imagine it. We also get an emotional connection, because we're seeing the charm of the dog and Marcus's lovable inability to not give it a treat.

With this in mind, this chapter is all about learning to decrease your word count to retain reader engagement and write a sharper book. Now you're getting used to the idea of cutting out words you don't need, let's get a little more specific on the words you or your editor may brutally cut (have you ever heard of killing your darlings?) to make your writing stronger.

Filler Words

You probably say a lot of filler words in speech. I definitely use lots of crutches like 'um', 'ah', 'like', or 'just'. But in fiction, depending on the context and voice, these weak words can be eliminated to keep your sentences shorter and sweeter. Fillers are *filler*. They don't add to the story, they just add to the word count. Getting on top of them can massively improve your writing.

For most writers, the biggest culprit is 'that'. It's so often not needed. I'd like you to read through a sentence from your manuscript including 'that'. Maybe you've written something like, *She could tell that he was worried*. If you say it aloud, *She could tell he was worried*, also makes sense. And notice how much better it flows this way, without an unnecessary word clunking up the middle of the sentence? Here's an example of cutting down a sentence by removing filler:

- 'They went to the shop **so that they could buy** lettuce.'

- 'They went to the shop **so they could buy** lettuce.'

- 'They went to the shop **to buy** lettuce.'

Here are some more filler words:

- **Had**: If you're already writing in past simple tense, you usually don't need it.

- **Literally/Actually/Definitely/Clearly**: Avoid

unless you really need to spell it out that something is true.

- **Very/Really**: Instead of adding this to an adjective, change the word completely. For example, 'very good' can be shortened to 'great' or even 'fantastic'.

- **Of/Just/So**: Similarly to 'that', read aloud the sentence and see if it can be deleted without impacting clarity.

If you find any of these in your manuscript, give them a good look and see if they can be omitted, or if the sentence could be reworked. Don't feel bad if you use a lot of them. Lots of us writers tend to, including me, and it's something we become mindful of over time. You don't have to delete every single one, but cleaning up the manuscript a bit can make a big difference. Using the Find or Search function on your writing software can help you identify your filler words more easily.

Adverbs

The idea of avoiding adverbs at all costs is one of the most common pieces of writing advice I see. Beginner writers especially have a reliance on them that slows down their writing. No, adverbs aren't the root of all evil, but in most cases, they can be omitted or swapped out to show instead of tell.

- **Adverb telling:** *'What's that?' she asked* disgust-edly.

- **Showing:** *'Ew, what's that?' She scrunched her face.*

- **Adverb telling:** *He went very quickly to the store.*

- **Showing:** *He sprinted to the store.*

In other cases, adverbs may be redundant next to the verb they're paired with, so they can be omitted:

- *Whispered quietly*

- *Yelled loudly*

- *Cried sadly*

All this said, don't delete your adverbs just to replace them with another redundant word or phrase. For example, *They spoke in a delicate sort of way*, is weaker than, *They spoke delicately*, so don't get fooled into changing all your '-ly' words without thinking it through.

Repetition

- *'Hello!' she exclaimed*

- *'Oh, no . . .' she trailed off.*

Does anything feel wrong to you in the above sentences? The unnecessary dialogue tags are just one example of repetition in writing. We know from the exclamation mark that the first piece of dialogue was exclaimed, and we know from the ellipses in the second that she trailed off. When we say something twice, even in different words, we're wasting space on the page and wasting the reader's time.

Repetition can also happen on a larger level, like when scenes feel too similar. Maybe you overuse the same describing words, pieces of dialogue, inner monologue themes, clichés, movements and expressions, or more. Many authors, for example, rely on common body language actions like eyebrow raises and shrugs. Or, they may have lines of inner monologue that repeat the same ideas over and over as the character mulls things over throughout the book – but just because they're rethinking the same things doesn't mean *we* need to hear the whole thing again and again.

Also reconsider using the same word twice in a paragraph when another could be used for variety. '*The flowers were a beautiful shade of pink. The dog sniffed at them with its little pink nose.*' Could we use a different word for 'pink' in one line? The roses might be a 'beautiful blushy shade', or the dog's nose could be 'rosy'. Repetition can cause the reader to catch on the words, but variation helps the writing flow.

Sometimes repetition can be okay. It can be used to nail down a concept to the reader, by showing how important it is to the character in that moment. *Fear was what he felt. Fear was all he knew. Fear trickled through his blood and froze his limbs.* In this case, it really shows the terror is consuming the POV character.

Overwriting

Overwriting usually happens when writers don't trust their readers' intelligence enough to leave some things up to subtext. Similar to repetition, it can lead to a sluggish book that feels as if it's being told or drilled into the reader's head. When overwriting becomes an issue, the reader gets bored and irritated, because you're spelling everything out in painful, patronising detail. Instead, we want to let them fall into the story naturally and enjoy it.

Jenny yawned. She was so tired. A long day at her job where she was an administrator, taking phone calls all day, left her without much energy by 5pm when it became her personal time again. She sat down in her chair and blinked her eyes. The TV played an old show, across from Jenny's chair where she could see it. She turned up the volume, though, in order to hear it a bit better. She felt so sleepy.

This example has a lot of overwriting, which slows down the pacing and wastes page space. Below are two of the most common cases of overwriting, so you can identify which I used in the above example.

I believe, I see, I think:

Lines like this are usually unnecessary, because we know we're in a character's head and therefore we know that if something is described, they're seeing it, feeling it, thinking it, etc. For example, *She thought it was strange how the curtains were closed, but she supposed it was late evening. Then she saw a flash behind the curtain and she felt a shiver run down her spine.*

We can simplify this, to: *How strange, that the curtains were closed! Although it* was *late evening. A flash behind the curtain sent a shiver down her spine.* This version puts us more deeply in the moment, has stronger character voice, and has a lower word count.

Shrug your shoulders, kick your foot, blink your eyes, nod your head:

These are examples of being told what body part is moving, when we already know because the verb shows us.

You can't shrug anything other than your shoulders, so the simpler 'you shrugged' is much more effective. This is especially important in fast paced scenes, as the fewer words used, the better the sense of urgency.

Let's look at the example of Jenny's evening again, this time with the overwriting removed. Here, I was able to take the paragraph from seventy-nine words to thirty-two. Imagine if you did that throughout your manuscript – the impact it could have!

Jenny yawned. A long day at her admin job left her without much energy. She sat in her chair and blinked. The TV played an old show, and she turned up the volume.

Sometimes, readers have the opposite problem: underwriting. If you feel your prose needs some more rounding out or is falling flat, I encourage you to go back to our chapter on the building blocks of prose: the description, action, inner monologue, and dialogue. Usually, this feeling of underwriting comes from an imbalance where a building block is missing.

Directions and speeds

Did you notice how I removed the sentence in Jenny's story above about how her chair faced the TV? We already know it must be facing the TV, or can easily assume so, if she's sitting in her chair watching a show. In this instance and many others, we can often infer directions and speeds from other, stronger parts of the writing, rather than telling the reader.

We also didn't need to know she 'sat down' in her chair, because sitting infers you're going downwards. 'She sat' is plenty. Often, directional words like up, down, back, and forward, aren't needed when the verb tells us enough about where someone or something is going. For example, we don't need to know someone is 'walking forward' because this is usually how people walk – however, 'walking backwards' would be clarified because this is uncommon. Similarly, phrases like 'on top of' or 'in order to' can be shortened to 'on' and 'to'.

Words that tell us the order or speed of events also aren't usually helpful. 'Then' or 'consequently' are not needed as we know that if a sentence follows another sentence, the second sentence is happening after the first.

Meanwhile, timing words like 'suddenly' or 'slowly' are weak adverbs that can be replaced with strong verbs, by showing, or by being more strategic with your sentence structure.

Things/Stuff

Words that are unspecific don't tend to be helpful to the reader. If you're relying on 'things' and 'stuff', make sure you're still giving enough specifics that the reader can imagine what's going on. Saying, *There's stuff every-where,* is telling, whereas describing what the stuff is and where it's placed is showing.

Tentative Language

We can omit most tentative words because they feel passive and describe something the character means to do – but not the actual action. This usually comes in the form of 'to'. For example, *She reaches up to cup his face so she can kiss him.* Because she isn't actually doing the action of cupping his face and kissing him, we're left at arm's length from the action. *She reaches up, cups his face, and kisses him*, feels more immersive.

Okay, so what are some good words?

The best word and phrase choices allow us to evoke voice, theme, and atmosphere. Let's say we're writing from the POV of a very happy character in a very happy moment, and we use the following: *Oliver saw the city before him, with skyscrapers and winding, busy roads. He couldn't wait to get in there and explore.*

This example is correct grammatically, but it uses redundancies, tells instead of shows, and doesn't utilise character voice. Let's try again: *The soles of Oliver's feet almost buzzed, wanting to carry him into the shining lights and busy streets. Yes, yes, yes! There was so much to do and see, all at his fingertips.*

Often, moving from bad words into good words can be solved by moving from telling into showing. 'Feet almost buzzed' and 'carry him' show Oliver's excitement. He's joyous, and ready to go! 'Shining lights' is a description

I used to evoke a sense of beauty and excitement. If I'd used something like 'glaring lights', it would instead show Oliver's dislike of the city, or give a sense of overstimulation rather than wonder.

Exercise: List your weaknesses

Now you know all the ways words can be 'bad', you might have already started thinking of ones you know you overuse. If not, now's the time to read through your manuscript and find your filler and redundancy weak points. You might also upload your manuscript online to a program that tells you which words you use most. If you've identified that you overwrite or have a lot of repetition, take note of that as well.

Try to format your list of weaknesses in a way that's helpful for you to refer back to. Print it out and stick it on the wall next to your computer as you do your copy editing. It can be difficult to remember everything, but having this easy sheet that reminds you what to look out for can massively help you. It can even be a section in your style sheet! Eventually, you'll find you get better because you've trained yourself to write without filler.

18

Spelling

As part of your journey through this chapter, I would like you to explore the best dictionary option for you and familiarise yourself with it. In Australia, one of the most popular dictionaries used across publications is Macquarie. A dictionary is a great resource for a writer, and even though some trusted online ones aren't free, I recommend choosing your favourite and getting a subscription. Remember that as an author, an expense like this can be used as a tax deduction, or you may be able to access an online dictionary for free with your library card.

This book *isn't* a dictionary, and for the most part, one will serve the purpose of figuring out how to spell words in your book. Whatever writing software you use will also do a lot of the work for you, between Spellcheck and AutoCorrect (but trust your gut and check if something feels off, since these can be wrong). Here, rather than teach you basic principles of spelling, I'm going to focus this chapter on common errors, considerations special to spelling in fiction, and other style sheet notes.

Homophones

Homophones are words that sound the same but have different spellings and meanings. Since they're easy to mix up, they tend to be the biggest spelling struggle for writers. While readers don't notice correct spelling, poor spelling will quickly turn them away. It's important to stay on top of these and know our weak points. Here are some common ones to keep an eye out for:

- **Two, To, and Too:** *Two dogs are going to the park, too.*

- **They're, Their, and There:** *They're seeing their parents over there.*

- You're and Your: *You're going to ruin **your** dinner.*

- Than and Then: *If you think you're better **than** me, **then** just leave.*

- Loose and Lose: *Your pants are so **loose** you might **lose** them!*

- Bear and Bare: *I can't **bear** to see your cold hands **bare** like that.*

- Affect and effect: *The light **affects** the colouring, creating a dappled **effect**.*

- Stationery and Stationary: *The **stationery**, unused, sits **stationary** on her desk.*

- Compliment and Complement: *She **compliments** the way the colour of my shirt **complements** my eyes.*

- Accept and Except: *I **accept** your terms, **except** for that one.*

British versus American

In Australia, we get most of our spelling and punctuation rules from UK English, but with so much US media, many writers get confused. With every English-speaking country having its own nuances in the use of the language, it's easy to end up in a jumble. There are quite a few differences between US and UK English, so no matter where you are, you need to always make sure you're writing correctly for your audience. Using a trusted dictionary for your country and ensuring your spellcheck is set to your country is key.

That said, many authors from outside of the United States still use US English, since it's such a big market in the publishing industry. Often, an author will make this decision because it means catering to the majority of their readers. As always, it's your choice to make, and consistency is most important. Find and Replace can help with many common Americanisms, since you can search for a word and check your spelling throughout the document. If you get confused, I recommend keeping a list next to you as you copy edit so you stay aware of your spelling.

In typical US English:

- '-ise' becomes '-ize' (realise versus realize)

- '-our' becomes '-or' (favour versus favor)

- '-re' becomes '-er' (centimetre versus centimeter)

For example:

- UK: *Have you **analysed** the **colours** for the **centre**?*

- US: *Have you **analyzed** the **colors** for the **center**?*

Remember also that different countries have different punctuation expectations. For example, in Australia it's common to use single quote marks, but in many other countries, double quote marks are more expected. Utilise your style sheet to make decisions and remain consistent.

Compound words

While contractions simply squish two words together with an apostrophe ('I've', 'there's'), compound words place two full words together, either without a space, with a space, or with a hyphen ('proof-reader', 'proof reader', or 'proofreader'). Because there's different ways to style them, it's super important that they show up in your style sheet so you stay consistent.

Step one is to make a general decision on whether your compound words will be hyphenated, and if they aren't hyphenated, if they'll be open or closed ('note book' or 'notebook'). Step two is to decide when your style gets to be broken. Compounding or un-compounding words can create clarity when there's ambiguity. For example, *I resent that*, is different to, *I re-sent that*. This is why it's so important to double check all your compound words during edits for readability.

You can also use hyphens to compound words when their meaning might be confused otherwise. For example, 'the small dog petsitter' reads differently to 'the small-dog petsitter' and 'a man-eating lion' has a different meaning to 'a man eating lion'. With hyphens, we're hearing about a petsitter for small dogs and a lion that eats people. Without them, we're hearing about a small dog that's a petsitter, and a man who's eating lion. Of course, we can usually assume what's correct, but in some cases it isn't so obvious (especially in SFF, where all sorts of things are possible), so compounding is a great tool for creating clarity.

Breaking rules of spelling

Using creative licence when it comes to spelling is typically more complex than breaking other writing rules, because the smallest deviation can change the entire meaning of a word. We risk readers becoming confused or being pulled out of the story. That doesn't mean it can't be done at all, though. As always, a bit of strategy and intention can make a creative choice shine.

Phonetic spelling (spelling words as they sound) is one way to do this, as it can be used to show someone's accent. Often, though, this is avoided, as it can be jarring to readers. An entire book written phonetically would be very difficult to read. But, to add flair to a character who only appears once or twice, it could do some helpful showing (though it's still often cautioned against, as this can get offensive very quicky). More often, phonetic spelling can be used to show when people are struggling to speak, for example if they're sick, their voice is muffled, they have food in their mouth, or they're struggling to pronounce a word. For example, *'This'ssogoood,' I mumble over a mouthful of pasta*, or, *Lara sniffled. 'Bore bainkillers, blease.'*

Slang, similarly, says a lot about a character. Some writers get caught up on slang words not being 'real' words, and wonder if it's considered wrong to use them. The problem is, slang can take a while to be added to the dictionary, but most people will still understand it. And this understanding is the most important part – as long as the reader gets it, it doesn't matter if it's a recognised English word. We often face the same problem with modern versus more traditional spelling, like 'alright' versus 'all right'. Some people will be adamant you can't use words and phrases that their dictionary disagrees with, but writing is creative for a reason!

Finally, you can break spelling rules by making up your own words. This is especially common in sci-fi and fantasy, in which writers are creating all sorts of unreal things. Why wouldn't the people in a fantastical world have some of their own language? Once more, making

sure the reader can still understand what's going on is
the key.

Exercise: Highlighting spelling

Let's do a super easy exercise for a nice breather! Grab a book from your shelf and pick a random page (ideally a book you've already read, so you don't accidentally see spoilers). Take a highlighter or some sticky notes and make a note any time you see a word that uses one of the spelling rules we talked about in this chapter:

- Homophones

- Compound words

- UK or US spelling

- Phonetic spelling

- Slang or made-up words

If you don't want to annotate in your book, type up the page but ensure you get the spelling exactly the same. Once you've noted all the instances where the author has made a spelling choice, think deeply about how they use spelling for clarity, emphasis, or to appeal to their audience. Do you believe they've done so well, or might you have made different choices?

Now, think over the spelling in your book. Have you used it strategically, clearly, and stuck to a consistent style?

19

Punctuation

In creative writing, punctuation use can vary greatly to serve a story and the character's voice. It keeps sentences flowing, engaging the reader and showing the tone of a scene. Using punctuation not just correctly but effectively is another huge part of writing, and as you edit, it's something to continue playing with. Each time we try something new or add a new punctuation skill to our toolbelt, our writing strengthens! In this book, I'd prefer to deep dive into common punctuation struggles for authors than cover all the basics of all punctuation marks, so for this chapter we'll be covering commas, apostrophes, colons and semicolons, and ellipses, as well as how to use punctuation to show, and where to break punctuation rules. *(P.S. We'll talk about punctuating dialogue in the dialogue chapter, so hang on just a bit longer for that.)*

Commas

We all know the basics: While full stops (or periods) are used to end a sentence, commas create pauses in between. They're the punctuation mark you'll likely use most, and since full stops, exclamation marks, and question marks are more self-explanatory, I'll skip right over those. Commas are a lot more complex.

Many new writers struggle with issues like run-on sentences and comma splices, because they don't quite understand where breaks should go. Sentences that sound natural when spoken aloud won't necessarily make sense on paper. Despite the sometimes confusing rules for commas, the most important trick is to read your sentences aloud, then rethink the writing:

- Where are the natural breaks in speech?

- Where can a comma increase clarity (e.g. an Oxford comma)?

- How many times have you already used conjunctions like *and*, that can keep a sentence going forever? Might you add a full stop instead, creating two shorter sentences?

- Can adding a comma bring rhythm to a sentence, or can removing one add a sense of urgency?

You'll find that all writers use commas differently, since they have their own tone that shines through their punctuation use. This is yet another reason it's so important to read widely. When you study how different authors use their commas, it helps you grow your own writing craft. Even better, you continue to improve when you practise using them in your own work to see how you can best blend your voice with strong clarity.

Rather than commas always needing to go in a specific place, they can move around to impact not just the flow but the meaning of a sentence. You may have heard the infamous, *Eats, shoots and leaves*, popularised by the highly-regarded punctuation book of the same name by Lynne Truss (2003). Of course, pandas eat shoots and leaves – they don't eat, then shoot, then leave!

When a comma is used in a list, it takes the place of 'and' or 'or'. *I went to my girlfriend's, Melissa's, then home.* Unless we already know who Melissa is, this list makes it unclear whether Melissa is the girlfriend, or if it's someone else's house the person went to before Melissa's. *I went to my girlfriend's, and Melissa's, then home*, or *I went to my girlfriend Melissa's, then home,* may be clearer. In lists, we also have the option to use an Oxford comma for clarity, which adds a comma before 'and' (this is my preference).

Commas are also used in pairs (where you might also use parenthesis or dashes, like I'm doing right here) to add information in the middle of a sentence. When you do this, the punctuation must always match, and you must both open and close the insertion. Without the insertion, the sentence should still be full and make sense, so the first part must agree with the second.

The following are all the same sentence, just with different punctuation or structure:

- *Shelly, who had very light hair, suited the brown hat.*

- *Shelly – who had very light hair – suited the*

brown hat.

- *Shelly had very light hair and suited the brown hat.*

- *Shelly suited the brown hat. She had very light hair.*

- *Shelly suited the brown hat because of her very light hair.*

Sometimes, whether or not we use comma pairs around insertions helps us understand the meaning of a sentence:

- *The people in the restaurant who had cake loved it.*

- *The people in the restaurant, who had cake, loved it.*

The first option's insertion of 'who had cake' tells us only some people had cake and loved it, but the second version tells us everyone in the restaurant had cake. This rule is known as 'defining', because the version without commas defines/narrows down who the noun refers to. With commas, however, we aren't defining a smaller subset of people but showing we're referring to them all.

We also use commas when we're naming someone to address them: *Jenny, what are we having for lunch?* or *Hey, Jenny!*

Remember to add comma choices to your style sheet where relevant. Some of these may be context dependent, but in general are a great indicator of your voice. For example:

- If you use an Oxford comma: *Beans, chips and cheese,* versus, *Beans, chips, and cheese.*

- If you add commas between clauses: *She was hot but she was wearing a jumper,* versus, *She was hot, but she was wearing a jumper.*

- If you add a comma before 'too' when used at the end of a sentence: *He's going to the park too,* versus, *He's going to the park, too.*

- If you add commas around time clarifications: *Then he went home,* versus, *Then, he went home.*

What's a comma splice?

This is the one major comma rule I want to warn you about, because comma splices are so prevalent in the writing of newer authors. They're wrong, and they're awkward, making for writing that's less readable. Take a look at these examples:

- **Incorrect:** *She's lying, she told me she did it!*

- **Correct:** *She's lying. She told me she did it!*

- **Correct:** *She's lying; she told me she did it!*

- **Incorrect:** *I walked to the shops, it took ages.*

- **Correct:** *I walked to the shops. It took ages.*

- **Correct:** *I walked to the shops and it took ages.*

Comma splices usually happen where there should be a full stop, semicolon, or conjunction, but the writer has used a comma to join two sentences instead. There are times, particularly in dialogue, where we can let a comma splice slide because it feels right with a character's voice. They offer a slurred effect, and may be useful in scenes where the character isn't fully focused, like when they're drunk or in an intense emotional state. Typically, though, comma splices are an error and should be avoided.

Apostrophes

There are a few reasons we use apostrophes: maybe we're using them for a contraction (like 'cannot' to 'can't'), maybe to show possession, or maybe for a direct quote. Like other forms of punctuation, they help to clarify the words we use, so knowing how to use them correctly is a huge part of creating a readable novel. The most common mistake I see with apostrophes is their use in plurals. Luckily, the answer is simple – don't use apostrophes for plurals!

Here are some examples of apostrophe use to help:

- **Wrong**: *I enjoy reading blog **post's**.*

- **Right**: *I enjoy reading blog **posts**.* (plural)

- **Wrong**: ***Thats** very interesting.*

- **Right**: ***That's** very interesting.* (contraction)

- **Wrong**: *Look at **Poppys** website.*

- **Right**: *Look at **Poppy's** website.* (possessive)

As usual, there's always exceptions to rules. 'It's' and 'its' are opposite, 'it's' being the contraction of 'it is', and 'its' being possessive! In this case, the contraction takes precedence and gets to keep the apostrophe for clarity. The possessive drops it so we can tell which is which. 'Who's' and 'whose' follow the same structure. Otherwise, *it's* literally that simple.

Any uses of apostrophes that are up to style will, of course, go in your style guide. For example, some writers prefer ''60's' rather than ''60s', or even ''60s' when referring to decades. But you may want to check the most common use in your country by looking at dictionaries or university websites.

Colons and Semi-Colons

If you struggle with these two, don't worry! Many people do, and it even took me a while to grasp the correct use. Although both are generally used to separate a sentence, colons come before a list or explanation, while semicolons are used to connect two clauses. The most common mistake I see is mixing up colons and semicolons in a list, like:

- **Wrong**: *We need several colours; purple, blue, red, yellow and pink.*

- **Right**: *We need several colours: purple, blue, red, yellow and pink.*

Semicolons have some great uses in English. You might choose to use them in a list for clarification when commas aren't enough: *We need several colours for the house: walls, pink; floors, brown; furniture, green; and windows, purple.* You can also often use a semi-colon to fix a comma splice, like, *She was really busy, her work was intense.* We could correct it to, *She was really busy. Her work was intense*, but the following flows better: *She was really busy; her work was intense.*

For the use of separating clauses, my advice is to avoid semi-colons if they aren't necessary and you're not sure they're right. Not only are they difficult for many people to use correctly, but they impact the readability of text because, like some of the other punctuation marks we've discussed, they aren't invisible in the same way commas and full stops are. You want your sentences active and engaging, and semi-colons can be jarring because readers aren't as used to them. But, if you can use them well, don't let me stop you; I know I love them. When editing your semicolons, ensure that on either side, the connected sentences can stand alone.

Ellipses

Ellipses are great for showing characters trailing off (remember this is different to being *cut* off, which we show with an em dash), or having a long pause as they think something over. Sometimes writers get a little confused about how they should be stylised and how the capitalisation around them works.

First, an ellipsis in fiction is always three dots. Never two, never four, never you just pressing down the full stop key on your keyboard a few times and doing whatever you feel like. Always. Three. You might be surprised how many unedited books have an incredible variation on this. Otherwise, you can do the spacing however you like – as long as it's consistent throughout the manuscript, like:

- *She was right there . . . At least, I thought she was.*

- *She was right there...At least, I thought she was.*

- *She was right there... At least, I thought she was.*

- *She was right there ... At least, I thought she was.*

Take a look at how I capitalised the second sentence in the above examples. A common error with ellipses is capitalising the following word after them incorrectly. Luckily, this is another one of those rules that's secretly super easy. We know an ellipsis either goes in the middle of a sentence, showing a long pause between words, or goes at the end of a sentence, showing a character trailing off. We also know that capital letters go at the beginning of a sentence, not the middle.

Therefore, if you're showing a break in between a sentence, you won't capitalise the first letter in the second half. But, if you're moving onto a new sentence after the ellipsis, you'll start with a capital letter just like you would with any new sentence. Like:

- **Wrong**: *Erin is so pretty . . . apparently she uses expensive mascara.*

- **Right**: *Erin is so pretty . . . Apparently she uses expensive mascara.*

- **Wrong**: *This coffee is . . . Disgusting!*

- **Right**: *This coffee is . . . disgusting!*

Punctuation that shows

Punctuation can be used in fiction to show emphasis and pace, like how ellipses show a thought or piece of dialogue trailing off. An exclamation point lets us give impact! A question mark shows us something is being asked. Dashes let us insert information in an easy-to-understand way. You may even use formatting creatively, like ALL CAPS TO YELL, or *italics for emphasis.*

These are all great techniques, but I want to also give you a word of caution. Using punctuation that isn't invisible too much is pretty exhausting on the reader, and also brings down the level of impact. IF YOUR CHARACTER SHOUTS EVERYTHING IN CAPS ALL THE TIME, the noise loses its effectiveness. Similarly, too many dashes can be distracting – because they pull the reader aside for a second – just to provide extra information – rather than letting the sentence flow.

Punctuation outside of our usual commas, full stops, and apostrophes can sometimes be distracting and slow down your story. We have to use just a tiny bit extra brain power to take them in. That means we want to use them only when they have impact – letting our writing speak for itself, rather than relying on too many tricks.

Breaking rules of punctuation

Particularly in dialogue, your characters will speak a certain way that doesn't always follow writing rules. Perhaps they talk fast, skipping commas, or their sentences sometimes jumble together incoherently. This comes down to tone and context. If you want your writing to be snappy, avoid excess commas. If you want it to be flowy and descriptive, don't be afraid of some interesting punctuation paired with longer sentences. The most important thing to remember is that your writing must still make sense to the reader. Read your work aloud, and with realism in mind, decide strategically where punctuation should be placed – 'correct' or otherwise.

Exercise: Reading aloud

It's amazing how much our work can change between writing sessions when we're writing what comes to us in the moment and not necessarily writing with strategy. We might feel out scenes differently on different days, or be influenced by the media around us, making our sentences come out in unexpected ways.

For this exercise, pick a page from your book and rewrite it entirely – but with no punctuation (except apostrophes, so it doesn't get too confusing). Then, with the original and the punctuation-free version in front of you, have a Text-to-Speech program (in Word or otherwise) read both out to you. Better yet, have a real person read it. Notice the ways both versions are read differently aloud when you don't punctuate natural pauses.

Then, without looking at the original version, add your punctuation back in. Try not to remember what you did originally, but punctuate in the way it feels right in this moment. Once you've done so, compare the original version and this new version. Has much changed? Did you make different choices this time, or were they very similar? You could have this version read aloud as well, and see which version matches the rhythm, tone, and voice best for the POV character and the context of the scene.

This exercise is about learning what your voice is like – seeing where you put your pauses, how your sentences flow, and what's most effective. Get the most out of this exercise by analysing your punctuation use deeply and considering where your strengths and weaknesses may be.

20

Dialogue

Definitions

- **Dialogue:** A subcategory of quoting, in which a character is saying something aloud or characters are engaging in a conversation and their direct speech is shown with quote marks.

- **Dialogue tag:** The 'she said' or similar that pairs with a piece of dialogue and tells us who spoke and how.

We're going to dedicate the next two chapters just to dialogue, because it's one of the biggest parts of fiction writing – and yet one people so often struggle with. How do you punctuate it? How do you make it sound real? Is 'said' *really* dead?

Punctuation in dialogue

Although it's something many new writers struggle with, punctuating dialogue is actually pretty easy! You probably already know that dialogue uses apostrophes as quotation marks (they may be single ' or double " depending on your country – in Australia we tend to use singles). If you have a quote within a quote, however, you'll use the opposite, for example: *'Mum was so mean this morning! She said, "Clean your room right now, or there'll be trouble!"'*

The main thing you need to know is that in fiction, **punctuation goes inside the quote marks:**

- **Correct:** *'Hi there,' she said.*

- **Incorrect:** *'Hi there' she said.*

- **Incorrect:** *'Hi there', she said.*

If you aren't using a dialogue tag, finish the quote with a full stop, not a comma, to indicate the end of a sentence, like, *'Hi there.'* If you are using a dialogue tag, consider it part of the sentence and use commas inside the quote marks instead.

Because writing is never too simple, *sometimes* punctuation doesn't go inside the quote marks in dialogue, but this is typically only seen in US English conventions. Although many dialogue style decisions will depend on your country or audience, ultimately decisions like this are up to you and your style sheet. As always, consistency is most important.

Occasionally, there'll be a piece of dialogue that isn't a full quote, and the rules also become a little less clear. Sometimes for a partial quote, we'll drop the comma or full stop, as well as any capital letters (except for proper nouns), to show it isn't a full sentence, for example:

- *Laurrie told me to 'pack it up', but I wasn't done yet!*

- *They called it her 'big break' because of how popular she got.*

- *And I said back that it 'isn't like that at all'!*

Interrupting speech with action

This is one that so many writers – and even editors – get wrong. I see it all the time, even in traditionally published books. For some reason, there seems to be misinformation about how to interrupt dialogue with an action beat. Maybe the tide is changing towards being more relaxed with this rule, but I'm still going to teach you about it, because I *hate to see it broken.*

The rule: Commas are only to be used at the end of dialogue when a dialogue tag is involved. Otherwise, you need stronger punctuation. When you interrupt speech with action, commas are not 'strong enough' and dashes or ellipses (whichever way you have chosen to consistently style them) are needed instead, like:

- **Wrong**: *'Hey, are you,' she stopped to think over her next words, 'free tonight?'*

- **Right**: *'Hey, are you—' she stopped to think over her next words '—free tonight?'*

- **Right:** *'Hey, are you'—she stopped to think over her next words—'free tonight?'*

- **Right:** *'Hey, are you . . .' she stopped to think over her next words '. . . free tonight?'*

- **Right:** *'Hey are you,' she said, stopping to think over her next words, 'free tonight?'*

When we're interrupting halfway through a line to add action (in the example, her stopping to think over her words) we can't use commas. Again, commas are for dialogue tags only – which we can see in the final example that adds a 'she said'. Otherwise, we have to show that the action is *interrupting* by introducing stronger punctuation.

Dialogue tags

Dialogue tags are a major part of your writing, but many new writers struggle to use them in an engaging way. Each of your characters should have their own voice and opinions, to the point where a reader should usually be able to tell who's talking without being told. Dialogue must always feel real and have purpose – so, what's the purpose and ideal use of dialogue tags?

It's generally recommended to use dialogue tags sparingly and keep them simple. Don't over-describe what the dialogue sounds like, but let it speak for itself by showing instead of telling. Like we talked about with redundant words to cut, too much description and dialogue tagging can distract the reader. If they can understand the speech on its own, you can save space on the page by cutting out redundancies in your dialogue tags.

Using 'said'

When first learning to write (especially in school), we're taught to use various dialogue tags. In one conversation your character might exclaim, then shout, then whisper, then cry, etcetera, etcetera, etcetera . . . As children, teachers want us to expand our vocabulary and learn different ways to describe things. Because of this, so many authors get caught up in trying to find unique and interesting dialogue tags, and trying not to use the same ones too often. 'Said' is villainised as boring and uncreative.

In most editor's and publisher's opinions, however, a simple 'said' is almost always preferred. Why? Because it's invisible. Our eyes skip right over 'said' because we're so used to seeing it, and like we've discussed with not overusing less common punctuation, we want to minimise how often the reader is reminded they're reading and not experiencing. 'Said' may not be as inventive, but it's more engaging. Using complicated terms is a distraction to your reader, when in most cases, you want them to be so lost in the story they forget they're reading. They have an imagination, and you shouldn't underestimate it, especially with the power of showing in your toolbelt. If they can infer how something was said, they don't need to be told.

In general, dialogue tags aren't always needed, especially complicated tags, and tags with adverbs are considered by some to be criminal. Yet sometimes we do need that extra clarification. Maybe your characters need to be distinguished more clearly in a conversation, or they're speaking differently to what we're used to. For example, if a character says something that could sound cruel but it's only a joke, you may want to mention that, so the reader isn't confused: *'You look disgusting,' she said sarcastically. 'Of course you look amazing, you idiot!'*

Dialogue that shows

Look at how the mood switches with these different greetings, no dialogue tags necessary:

- *'Oh. You're here.'*

- *'You're here!'*

- *'You're here?'*

- *'You're . . . here?'*

- *'You—I didn't think you'd make it!'*

- *'Um, hello, I guess.'*

As you edit your book, carefully read each dialogue tag and decide if it's needed. Is it clear who's speaking without it? If it's unclear, or the tone is unclear, might an action beat be more engaging to tell us who's talking? Action beats tell us who's talking because we know that only one speaker can appear in one paragraph. Since the named character is performing the action, we know the dialogue is also theirs. This makes action beats an often more engaging option than dialogue tags.

Donna stirred the pasta. 'I don't know. I guess I thought he'd be more . . .'

Sammy sprinkled in some basil. 'Tall?'

'Hm. It's not a dealbreaker, but he was a little . . .'

'Dry?'

Donna poured some more water from the kettle into the pot. 'Exactly.'

In this example, there are no dialogue tags, but we always know who's talking because of the action beats. In the sentences with no action beats, we know who's talking because in a conversation between two people, each line means we're going from one speaker to the other. It's like two people hitting a tennis ball back and forth over a net – we know they take turns. In your manuscript, are there places where you could use dialogue and action beats to show, rather than use dialogue tags to tell?

Capitalisation

You'll always start with a capital letter within a full quote, but never in the dialogue tag. This is still true when punctuation other than a comma is used, for example a question mark or ellipsis. The dialogue tag is always considered part of the same sentence as the dialogue. Of course, when we use an action beat instead of a dialogue tag, it will have a capital letter to start as it's a full sentence.

- **Incorrect**: *'Are you going to eat that?' She asked.*

- **Correct**: *'Are you going to eat that?' she asked.*

- **Incorrect**: *'She was like, um, you need to "Go home" or whatever.'*

- **Correct**: *'She was like, um, you need to "go home" or whatever.'*

In the second example, "go home" is not given a capital letter, since it's not a full sentence. On the other hand, if you're using the character's name in the dialogue tag, you will use a capital letter since it's a proper noun. *'Really?'* *Marvin asked,* but, *'Really?' asked Marvin.*

Formatting

Many new writers make the mistake of formatting an entire conversation in one paragraph. As we talked about under dialogue tags, we know that each line means a new person is speaking. This helps us distinguish who's talking, and gives us more of that lovely white space that helps keep the reader engaged – as opposed to a huge block of confusing, muddled dialogue.

All you have to do is go to a new line each time the speaker changes, or when the focus shifts away from the dialogue. You can also break up a long monologue by separating it into several paragraphs. This, again, helps us avoid huge chunks of text that don't let the reader breathe. The rule here is to start the new paragraph with a quote mark, but not use a quote mark to close the previous paragraph. This tells the reader that the same person is still talking. Of course, you can also break up monologues with some action or internal monologue to keep the reader engaged.

Exercise: Dialogue and action

Take a page or scene from your book that's heavy in dialogue, and Copy and Paste it into a new document so you can play with it. Check over your punctuation, and that every time a new character speaks, it's on a new line.

Now, within the dialogue, practise adding in action and description to break up the speech, until you have a strong blend of both elements. You can also add in more description and inner monologue, but for the purpose of this exercise, I want you to primarily focus on how action can liven up dialogue.

How have your changes affected the scene? Does adding more elements to your dialogue-heavy page make the scene stronger, or weaker?

Next, try the opposite. Remove everything except the dialogue, including the dialogue tags. Looking at your dialogue alone, how does it stand? Does the dialogue show enough that you can understand who is speaking, and the tone they're speaking with, even without it being told? How might you edit the words your characters use to make their dialogue show more?

21

Is the Dialogue Realistic?

We're so close to mastering dialogue! All we need to learn now is how to polish it and make it so good readers won't notice it isn't real. They'll feel so pulled into each conversation it'll be like they're actually hearing it. If dialogue should always push the narrative forward with clear purpose, how do we make that happen?

Does the dialogue add to the story?

This is the first check you should make when writing or editing your dialogue, because if your dialogue isn't needed, it's got to go! Is the quote you're using going to move the story along, tell the reader something about the character, or be otherwise engaging? If not, bye! Even if you love it, if the reader doesn't gain something, they'll be more likely to lose interest in the book.

You may remember that when we talked about effective chapters, we learnt the concept of starting and ending in the action. This is why, in dialogue, we don't often see small talk – because even if it's a realistic part of a normal conversation, it adds nothing to the story. Long conversations that take time on 'how are you' and 'nice weather' aren't valuable. Unless, of course, they tell us something important. If the dialogue in your book is heavy on unimportant information, see how you can use your page space to deepen your characters' dynamics and show the reader more about them instead.

Does each character have a unique voice?

We all talk in our own way, and I'm not just talking about our accents. Our personalities and backgrounds affect how we talk, as well as the influences of the people around us. We all also have our own tone and opinions. This should be true for characters as well, and it's how we reach the point where readers can tell who's talking without relying on dialogue tags.

Most character voices come from a place of common sense more than any real complex strategising. A city influencer will talk pretty differently to a weathered outback farmer. Then there's realism factors like age. We wouldn't have a kid say, *'Greetings, Mother. What will we consume for breakfast today? I am very hungry.'* That doesn't sound authentic at all, unless you want to show the kid is secretly an alien – or having fun pretending to be one. Something like, *'Morning Mumma, what're we havin'?'* sounds more childlike.

The best advice here is to speak with real-life people who are similar to your characters, and study how they talk. Really listen. What words do they use? How do they craft their sentences? Do they put emphasis on certain words? What's their body language as they talk? What biases do they filter their opinions through, and what are they open about compared to what they're more closed off about? And, of course, how can you carry what you've learned over to your book?

Also consider context of each scene, particularly the other characters involved. As real humans, we often use different language around our family compared to our friends or coworkers. At a more intense level, this is known as code-switching, which typically concerns the language changes people use when their family has a very different culture than the people they talk to outside the home. But, even taking this concept simply, most characters will sound pretty different when they're in a university class compared to when they're drunk with their friends at the club. The way a character bends to these social expectations tells us a lot about who they are. As you edit your book, take note of whether or not your dialogue shifts with the realistic expectations of the context the characters are in.

Reading dialogue aloud

I've said this before and I'll keep saying it. Reading your work aloud – especially your dialogue – allows you to hear it in a new way. As I mentioned with cutting small talk, cutting the unrealistic talk is important too, and reading dialogue aloud will help you realise if it's something someone would actually say.

Sometimes we make a character say something because it helps the story, but it might just not be realistic. A character isn't going to stand there and give all the right words and answers. (For example, in movies where the villain tells the hero their entire evil plan . . . for no reason.) As authors, we have to be more strategic than that, and get across information in ways that feel authentic to readers.

Don't only read aloud your own work. Read other books in your genre, with similar characters to your own and a similar target audience, and study the dialogue. How does it flow? Does it sound realistic to you? Does it still work when read aloud, or do you have criticisms? What has the author done to make it engaging, or what have they failed to do?

Exercise: Playing with voice

Pick a short event that happens in your book and write out a brief timeline. Dot points can help with this as you move from the start – like arriving at a theme park – to the end – like hopping off a rollercoaster to be sick.

Now, I want you to pretend each major character in your book has personally experienced this event, and have each of them explain, as if they were speaking, what happened to them. From each of their points of view, and in each of their styles of dialogue, write out their version. This can either be the scene in their POV, or them literally telling the story to someone. Aim for less than 500 words each, unless you feel like going for more – I don't want to overwhelm you.

With your different versions in front of you, compare what makes each unique. How does the sentence structure change? The slang? Do they notice different things, or draw more attention to certain emotions than others?

You can also try having a character tell the story to another character, and then to a third different character. This can help you see how they might change their language for different audiences. For example, if they're explaining why they were late to their boss, the story would sound very different to how they explain it to their best friend.

22

Self Editing Methods

Holy moly, you made it to the end! You know all the things to look out for when editing your novel, from the top of the funnel with your characters and plot, right to the bottom with the tiniest pieces of punctuation. But that's a pretty overwhelming amount of things to now go through your manuscript and implement, isn't it? How do you actually get started? In this chapter, I'm going to suggest some well-loved self editing methods you might employ for your novel to help you not just get your editing done, but enjoy it!

Outlining

If you haven't already done so, going back and creating a chapter-by-chapter outline for your manuscript will help you see the overall arcs and plotlines better, allowing you to do better structural edits. I know this isn't the first time I've mentioned this, but I really want to reiterate it because it's so important. Your outline also helps you keep things more clean, organised, and consistent. Remember that you can use the same spreadsheet I use for free – just grab it from the link in the 'Resources' section of this book.

Take time away

This one is super easy, because it's just doing nothing! Pull back from your manuscript for at least a couple of weeks (the longer the better) after each draft. You want to forget as much of your story as possible between rounds of edits, so you can better identify where things aren't coming across the way you intend them to. Getting space also helps you think more like a reader than an author. It gives you a stronger ability to identify how engaging or entertaining the storytelling is. A fresh perspective is key to effective self editing.

Read it out loud

This is another great way to get space from your manuscript. Read it aloud, have someone else read it to you, or use a Text-to-Speech function. Not only is this great for making sure dialogue is realistic (like we touched on earlier), but it's a great way to get a good feel for your voice across all the writing elements. Reading out loud helps you make sure your punctuation is placed naturally and helps you identify awkward sentences. It will also show you where the tone feels off, for example if the writing is coming across too formal and should be more conversational.

Kidnap your darlings

The writing world calls the harsh task of omitting beloved lines or scenes from your work 'killing your darlings', but I disagree with throwing away good work. Yes, sometimes we have to cut something we love because it isn't right for the story we're telling. We do have to be brutal as self editors. But that doesn't mean you need to kill good work. Instead, I suggest kidnapping it and keeping it for a rainy day. Keep a document to the side for pieces of writing to try using elsewhere. Sometimes, we can even use deleted scenes as short stories or bonus chapters, which are great for marketing. It would be a waste to delete them.

Switch up the medium

To help you get a wider perspective on your work, change the way you read it by using a different medium. Like reading aloud, this helps you experience the manuscript in a new way, increasing your distance to help you view it more objectively. Try:

- Printing it

- Converting it to an ePub file and reading it as an eBook

- Changing the font (Comic Sans in a large pt can be fantastic for this – the sillier the better)

- Changing the background colour

You can also make changes to your editing routine for distance. If you usually write at your desk, try an editing session from the sofa. Or, try editing on another device in another location. Go to the library so you can use a different computer, or work off your phone from an outdoor space.

Find your most-used words and phrases

Using a program that helps identify the words you use most will help you find your crutches and create a more varied manuscript. Words that are very common like 'the' aren't going to be a problem, but you'll quickly see how often your characters are blinking, for example, or how often you bring up their *stormy grey eyes*. Please be cautious first, however, that any program you upload your writing into doesn't take any permissions to use your work, including for training AI.

Take notes first, then do your edits

Sometimes editing can feel overwhelming when there's so much to do, so you might want to first go in with a highlighter and colour code sentences you notice you need to change. For example, when you find an adverb, highlight it pink; when you find telling instead of showing, highlight it yellow; and when you find repetition, highlight it blue. This way you can identify what needs to change first, then go back in and make the alterations later when you're less overwhelmed. You can do things one at a time to make the editing process far less intimidating – you don't have to do everything at once.

Make sure you're having fun

If writing and editing is starting to feel like a chore, you probably need to pull back and make it fun again. You may have your own ways of reinvigorating your inspiration, but here are some of my favourite ones:

- Create a Pinterest board

- Create a playlist

- Visit a location for research

- People watch

- Read other books

- Rest

Remember that all counts as work when it comes to writing. Getting inspired is all part of the job, so let yourself wander and dilly dally if your process requires it.

'Cheat' with a grammar app

You can sign up to a free grammar program like Grammarly easily, and it picks up lots of smaller mistakes. This can be a great starting off point, and you can begin to see trends in your most common errors. Remember, however, to always have caution when giving any program your work. If there is any risk of it stealing your writing, avoid it.

Also, use your discernment as a writer. These tools correct your work with computer systems that lack context. They're particularly bad for sentence structure and tone of voice, especially when it comes to creative writing and fiction. Double-check everything before correcting, and if you're unsure, google it, check your dictionary, or check your style sheet. Remember – your voice is not always supposed to be 'correct'!

23

More Steps Before an Editor or Querying

Getting a manuscript prepared for professional editing or querying is more than doing all you can to get the text right. We can bring in others for feedback to continue improving our work even more, and we can also format the Word document and check it so it meets industry standards.

Formatting to-do list

The following may seem nitty gritty, but getting these formatting tasks done will either save your editor time (and therefore you money) or show publishers and agents that you're serious and understand industry expectations:

- Font in Times New Roman 12 pt, double spaced, and black.

- Double spaces deleted using Find and Replace.

- Any common errors checked with Find (not Replace, unless you're very confident about the change). Also check any possible errors carried from previous drafts, such as names that have been changed.

- Indents 1.25cm first line only on all paragraphs, except the first paragraph in a section/chapter.

- Margins 2.54cm or 1 inch on every side (usually default).

- Chapter titles styled as headings (e.g. Heading 1 in Styles) for ease of navigation.

- Any in-line notes you've left for yourself cleaned up (e.g. 'describe eye colour here'), with Comments and Track Changes deleted unless they're important for your editor to see.

- Title page at the start of the document including the name of the book, your name, the word count, and the genre.

- If querying, check the agent or publisher's submission guidelines and follow them exactly. Not doing so will likely result in a rejection before they've even read your work.

Beta readers

Beta readers aren't editors; they're more like test subjects, and they're typically unpaid (they just love reading and want to help you). They read your manuscript in its early stages and provide feedback on various aspects of your story. They can be friends, fellow writers, or members of your writing community who are willing to offer constructive criticism.

Engaging beta readers is one of the best things you can do for your manuscript. Many authors will use beta readers before professional editing and proofreading to make sure their audience will resonate with their book. Plus, because betas bring a fresh set of eyes to your manuscript, they can spot plot holes, inconsistencies, and areas where the story might need further development. Their unfiltered feedback helps you identify and address weak points.

Finding and selecting beta readers

I have a great writing community on social media, which is where I find my beta readers. This is another reason why it's so important to talk about your book and make connections with both people in the industry and potential readers long before you publish. You want to create a community that can help you in return for you helping them. If you're starting at square one, though, beta readers can be found in many places. Facebook groups for writers, especially, tend to have many beta readers floating around in them looking for books to read.

Although I have a database of beta readers that I've collated over the years, and a pretty solid small group that I trust, I almost always post to my Bookstagram (Book Instagram) or Booktok (Book TikTok) community to ask who's interested. Creating a team you can trust takes a lot of work and time, but it's well worth cultivating. You might even reach out to local book clubs or libraries. It's always a good idea to shake up your team and add new faces for fresh feedback, or remove people whose feedback isn't proving to be helpful.

Make sure you choose betas who are part of your target audience, not just other writers or friends. Selecting beta readers from your readership allows you to gauge how well your story resonates with the people you intend to captivate. They should be readers of your genre, enjoy the tropes in your book, and be in the right age group. The right readers' insights can provide valuable guidance on whether your characters are relatable, your pacing is engaging, and your overall storyline is compelling. And most importantly, you want to use beta readers who you can trust to be kind but also honest.

Working with betas

Unfortunately, a lot of people are unreliable. Since they're usually helping you for free, you can't expect too much from your beta team. I usually say that if you get ten beta readers for your book, expect to only hear back from five, and out of that, expect only valuable feedback from three.

Creating your ideal feedback team for your author journey might take a few books (there'll be people you need to weed out, for example if they don't return feedback on time, or if their feedback is rude and unhelpful) but the right team is invaluable, especially if you want to be a career author and continue producing books. Yes, there will be beta reader nightmares. But trust me, the good ones are worth the trouble of the bad ones!

When you're using beta readers, be incredibly clear on your expectations. Set a due date at least two weeks before you actually need the feedback, because trust me, a lot of them will be running late. Send out reminders intermittently and check up on how their reading is going. Don't spam them, though. More than one or two emails a week would be too much. It can be tricky to balance micro-managing with keeping betas on top of their work, but you'll figure it out in time.

Questions for beta readers

It's usually best to ask specific questions to guide their feedback. Don't ask anything too complex, because beta readers aren't professionals. Instead, ask about the basics, like if they thought the plot flowed well and if they liked the characters. What did they feel worked, what needed some improvement, and what in general did they like or dislike?

You may choose to send out a full questionnaire (this is my preferred method) to help get the specific feedback you want. *Did the main character's motives make sense to you? Was the worldbuilding clear? Was character X's dynamic with character Y realistic?* And, always ask for positive feedback – *What did you enjoy most?* – you'll want it!

24

Working With an Editor

The idea of this book has been to empower you to get ready for editing (or querying, which we'll discuss in the next chapter), so that when you hire an editor, their workload is lessened, your voice can remain strong, and overall you'll save money on editing costs. Now we've finished talking about self editing, I want to dedicate a chapter to talking about the process of working with an editor. How do you find one, and how do they work?

Though some people will read this book and go on to not use an editor since they feel they can cover everything on their own, that's not at all what I want you to get out of this. Although editors can be expensive, a good one is absolutely worth their fees. They will ensure your book is up to standard and your readers will enjoy it, but they'll also teach you to improve your craft so your skills keep getting stronger. I'll always advocate for the important work we editors do.

Consider your needs before hiring an editor. We talked about the types of editors earlier in this book, and I encourage you to refer back so you can really think on what's best for you. Here are some ways to find editors:

- Looking in the acknowledgements sections of books.

- Searching on LinkedIn.

- Searching on Facebook, Instagram, and TikTok.

- Searching the databases of editing association websites.

- Googling for a niche specialist, e.g. *YA fantasy editor Australia.*

Reedsy can be another good source, as its purpose is to be an editor-specific database. But please always be cautious, even if an editor on there looks amazing. Just because someone has worked on some major titles doesn't mean they're the best for you. I've seen people be scammed by Reedsy editors, meanwhile many amazing editors aren't granted access due to the site's high standards. Always, always check for real testimonials and get a sample edit to make sure an editor is best for you – no matter what qualifications and experience they may have.

On the other hand, platforms like Fiverr and Upwork have a lot of editors who offer extremely cheap rates. These editors are typically not professionals, and if they claim to be, vet them thoroughly. It's usually telling when someone says they're skilled but are charging far less than minimum wage. There are real editors on these websites, and some do have low fees, but always be cautious. Remember that editing rates are usually based on your manuscript length and genre, as well as the extent of editing required. If someone's rates are unusually high or low without good reason, consider it a red flag.

Here's an example of how the professional editing process may work:

1. The author completes their manuscript to the best of their ability.

2. The author researches different editors.

3. The author reaches out to a chosen few editors to ask for sample edits and quotes.

4. The author receives back samples and quotes, and from them picks the editor who is the best fit.

5. The editor books the author into their schedule. (Some editors are very busy and get booked out well in advance, so you may want to start looking for editors at least three months before you will actually use them). Usually at this time, the author will pay a deposit to book their spot – typically 50% of the overall fee – and a contract will be signed to protect both parties.

6. The author sends their manuscript to the editor, having clarified the type of edit that will be done, and how much back-and-forth will be involved. For example, will there be one or two passes? Will coaching be involved, including follow up calls?

7. The author sits impatiently and waits for the edits to come back, taking themself on long mental health walks to stop ruminating.

8. The editor sends the edits back, and the author goes through them and decides which to accept. At this point, the editor will send the final invoice and the author will pay for their service.

How important are sample edits?

You want to make sure you're choosing someone who is not only skilled in editing, but who can work with your manuscript, work with *you*, and who can offer a quote within your budget. Sample edits allow writers and editors to decide if they should work together, and allow writers to know that the editor they're choosing is reliable. I'm always, always going to shout about how vital they are.

Getting to know your editor

Sample edits aren't just about seeing if the editor is 'good'. If you've found an editor you like the sound of and are at the point of asking for a sample, I'm sure you've already noted that they have great reviews, a portfolio, and a strong knowledge of your genre. You wouldn't choose them otherwise.

A sample is really about seeing how the editor works with *your* manuscript, and how they work with *you.* Are their suggestions clear, empathetic, and helpful? Are their suggestions in line with the service you've hired them for/are they meeting your expectations? Do they look at many aspects of the work, such as noting where dialogue feels unrealistic, or are they only correcting major errors? And, what do *you* want them to look at most?

Editing is a big job that takes many hours and a lot of communication, so if you don't match with the personality and style of your editor, you're going to run into problems. It is really difficult for most writers to put their work out there, especially for professional criticism. If the sample edit shows that the editor is not respectful of you and your style, and instead is unkind in their comments and imposes their style over your own, it isn't a good match. Similarly, if you don't get along over phone or email, it will be a tough relationship.

Sometimes, as an editor, I see a manuscript that doesn't work with my style at all, and I know I'll have a lot of trouble working on it. Not because it's a bad manuscript, but because it is extremely far from my preferences. When this happens, I typically pass on it – even if it means me losing money. I want editing to always be an enjoyable and valuable experience for myself and the client. If I dislike what I'm editing, it'll shine through in the quality of my work. Always, always use your sample edit to see how you like the personality of the editor and how they respond to your work.

Getting a quote

Asking for and receiving quotes for editing is scary. Spending money often is, and editing tends to cost a lot more than most writers expect. This is because it takes a *lot* of time, effort, skill, and education. If the editor is a freelancer, their fees also help them run their business. You might have heard creatives say 'passion doesn't pay bills', and this is very true. Editors need to be paid, and fairly.

Sample edits allow editors to make a good prediction of what the overall project will cost. Typically, an editor will compare the sample to the size of the whole book, multiplied by how much money they need to make hourly. So, if a sample of 1000 words takes them one hour (an average editing rate), they charge $60 per hour, and the author has told them the full manuscript is 80,000 words, the quote will come to $4800. That might seem like a lot of money, but consider that this edit will take them *80 hours*! It's a highly skilled job and it takes time – you don't want someone who's going to rush through it.

Professional editing is an investment in your author career. A book with confusing prose or distracting typos is difficult to enjoy, and certainly doesn't stand out from the crowd of well-polished books that are available. Skipping editing, or any other important phase of publishing, like professional design, is going to cost you long-term. Many authors realise this the hard way, which is why you see a lot of authors re-releasing old books with new changes and covers years later, or even rebranding entirely as an author due to backlash. The better the product you release, the better reception it'll receive, the better reviews, and therefore the more sales you'll make. It helps you in the short and long term.

Note: All editors and genres are different, so individual research is important. For a list of standard editing fees, look up your country's professional editing association.

Provide your sample from the middle of your book

Many editors request samples to come from the middle of the book, because this area is typically less well-edited by the author than the beginning or end. (As writers, we know how important the first few pages in particular are, and how much we tweak them until they're perfect.) I ask potential clients to send me the first chapter of their book, plus 1000 words from the middle. This way I can read the beginning to get context, and complete an edit on a section of the book that can give me a good idea of what the overall job will be like.

Don't obsess over your sample before sending it. Don't worry about impressing the editor, and certainly don't try to trick them with a sample that doesn't reflect your whole work. If the editor gives you a quote based on a sample that is far more polished than the rest of the book, you might be charged a lot more than you expected. That's why we ask for a middle scene.

Don't attempt the Franken-edit

Please, please don't try to scam editors by getting free sample edits from many of them and then putting the samples together for a free edit. The concept of a Franken-edit may sound ridiculous, and would certainly be a lot of effort, but people really do try it. You would have to ask so many editors for samples that you would certainly be caught and blacklisted. And, even if you managed it, every editor is different. That's why we call it a Franken-edit: each section of your book would be edited by someone else, giving it different levels of quality and style. The book would be a mismatched mess!

Readers will notice this, and they'll be distracted from your story. Remember, the point of editing is to get your work to the highest quality possible. Using tricky ways to get your edit done cheaper – including choosing the cheapest editor you can find without checking the quality of their work – will only mean your book will be worse off. If that's the case, you might as well not have it edited at all. Please use sample edits wisely and considerately.

Hey Poppy, I really liked this book, and I want to be an editor! Where do I start?

Wait, really? That's so exciting. I absolutely love editing as a career, and although like all jobs it has some down-sides, I'm so glad I've found something I'm so passionate about. I get to help people tell the stories of their hearts and create art – is there anything more amazing? Encouraging people to improve their craft, helping them become more confident, and getting people from all walks of life past the hurdles of publishing is my passion.

I touched on what an editor does in the early chapters of this book, including how I got into editing. I mentioned how you don't need a university degree, or even any quali-fications, though they certainly help. What you need most are a) a great eye for detail, b) to read a lot and read widely, and c) empathy and enthusiasm for helping people tell their stories.

A great way to get a taste of editing is to start by beta reading. By getting on beta teams, you learn to provide good feedback and pick apart a story to understand what's working and what isn't. This is also an awesome way to network and start making friends with newer authors – who will remember you down the line and hopefully bring you work.

Get really familiar with using style sheets (you might even find style sheets of different publishing houses or even major companies, or universities, to study), but also with the ways we sometimes break the rules. Editing takes a lot of creativity and thought in distinguishing what to correct or suggest and when.

You might also start getting experience by applying for internships with publishers – or even smaller publications like a local newsletter – to offer editing expertise, get experience, and learn. You can even write to new authors or small indie publishers and volunteer to proofread or edit their books for free in exchange for the experience (but be cautious with this, as you don't want to do too much free work and get taken advantage of).

Another great way to start getting into editing professionally is joining editing associations, which are in many countries and can offer courses, workshops, and accreditation in editing. This can also be helpful to authors who want to learn editing skills, even if they don't plan to become a professional editor. I'm very happy to be a member of IPEd, Australia's fantastic editing association

I wish you all the best in your editing journey! This is such a wonderful, rewarding industry, and you're going to love it here.

25

Querying for Traditional Publishing

Although the last chapter was about getting ready specifically for an editor, which you may do even if traditional publishing is your goal, let me now help you get an idea of querying. This can be a very scary and overwhelming journey to set out on, but remember first and foremost that we all started somewhere. Thousands of authors go through the querying process every year, and although it isn't easy, you're not alone.

Querying is the process of submitting your work to agents and publishers in the hopes of having your book traditionally published.

In Australia, unlike the US and UK, it's more common to approach publishers directly than to get an agent. Our industry is small, so we don't have many agents, and the ones we do have are usually not open for submissions since their lists are keeping them busy enough. However, across all countries, it's important to keep in mind that agents and publishers are often open and closed to submissions at different times. Further, even when they are open for submissions, they may only be looking for specific genres or even more specific tropes and themes.

Step one is to create a running list of agents and publishers, and never submit something against their guidelines or outside submission openings. Querying takes a really long time, and you have to be prepared for that before diving in. Remember that traditional publishing is extremely slow. If you start querying today, it's more likely than not that your book – if it is ever bought by a publisher – will take two years to be released. Be prepared for a long journey, and although goal setting is great, have lots of backup plans and ready yourself to try different strategies.

How do you get an agent or publisher?

First, you have to look for publishers and agents, and then you can begin submitting. To find those who might be interested in your book:

- Search the Manuscript Wishlist website.

- Search the QueryTracker website.

- Search #ManuscriptWishlist on social media.

- Search publisher websites and find their submissions page.

- Read the acknowledgements of books like yours to see who represents the book.

- Go to writing festivals and author events, and network with the people who attend.

- Enter pitching contests.

- Enter competitions run by publishers.

- Sign up to industry newsletters that share writing opportunities like submission openings.

If an agent or publisher requests your full manuscript, take this as a big compliment! It isn't a guarantee they'll sign you, but it says your book stood out and caught their attention. Sometimes, they might read the book then suggest you make some edits before resubmitting it (an 'R&R' or 'revise and resubmit'). In this case, it's totally up to you if you want to make those edits or look for representation elsewhere. Sometimes their suggestions will make the story much better – but it's your story and your choice. If you want to fight for something at any point in the publishing process, fight for it!

On the topic of standing up for yourself, there are scammers out there, so always be cautious. It's common to ask the agent or publisher to speak to other authors on their list, and if you get to the point of 'the call', ask lots of questions. It doesn't matter how prominent the agent or publisher is – this is a professional relationship and you'll be working together a lot, so make sure it's a good fit.

If they ever ask for money, *run.* In traditional publishing, unlike self publishing, money flows to you. Agents and publishers do the work 'for free' because they make money off your book, while you earn royalties. It's difficult in publishing when you have your hopes so high and want to believe everyone who says they want the best for you, but you should always be very careful. If someone says they'll be your agent for X money or will publish your book for Y money, stop and research them thoroughly.

Remember, also, that getting an agent or publisher is a really difficult thing to do. I'm sure I won't be the first person you've heard say this, but it's true that getting lots of rejections isn't necessarily a reflection of your skill as an author. This is a highly competitive industry, and there's a lot of luck in terms of finding the right person to publish your book at the right time. If the rejection is ever becoming too much, step back for a little while and get your confidence back so you can dive back in stronger than before.

The query letter

The biggest part of querying is the query itself, usually in the form of a 'query letter'. You don't just slide into an agent's DMs telling them you've got the next big thing and they should jump on it now before it's too late. There's a method to this, which enables us to put our best foot forward, and also for the agent to not get overwhelmed with nonsensical pitches.

Query letters are like a package you present to agents and publishers, which are often in the form of an email and include:

- Your hook

    ○ A one sentence elevator pitch for your story.

- A short description

    ○ Less than 250 words that tells us what the book is about – just the highlights.

- A sentence or two on why the agent or publisher might be interested

- Your author bio

    ○ Up to 250 words on who you are, why you're telling this story, and if you have previous writing experience or awards.

- Your synopsis/summary

    ○ A one page document that details the plot

of the story in full, with spoilers (this isn't a blurb).

- A sample of the manuscript

- Book details like: the word count, genre, age range, comp titles, or any other relevant information

In your query letter, always:

- Personalise to the agent or publisher (mention books on their list, for example, that make you think they'd like your book too).

- Don't be boastful about how great your book is. Let the query and manuscript sample speak for themselves.

- On the other hand, still be confident! Don't come across as desperate or self-deprecating.

- Show gratitude for their time.

There are countless resources online for putting together your query letter, so I advise researching to find specific examples that apply to you.

Tips for organisation

Since querying can take a long time, take a lot of different documents, and it's easy to accidentally forget who you've queried, when, and how, staying organised makes things much simpler. These are some common strategies:

- Keep all details in one document so it's easy to Copy and Paste into the agent or publisher's preferred submission format.

- Have copies of your manuscript that have the first three chapters, ten chapters, 10,000 words, etc. Different agents and publishers ask for different amounts all the time, and it's much easier to have these on hand so all you have to do is attach the file, rather than copy out a certain amount to a new document each time.

- Create a spreadsheet that details the agents/publishers you're submitting to, when you submitted to them, and if you hear back. Most authors will submit to at least 50 people, so keeping this organised is key. You don't want to accidentally query someone twice.

- Don't submit to everyone at once. Wait a while after each 'batch' to see if you get feedback that may improve your query for next time. Remember that not all agents and publishers are open at all times, so keep a timeline to remember when to submit to specific people.

26

Writing with Sensitivity

This wouldn't be a book on editing if I didn't talk about one of the lesser known but vital roles of editors before we end. Beyond improving prose and ensuring the book is realistic and accurate, we think of the people, experiences, and cultures you include in your work, and how well you portray them. Editors are the bridge between you and your audience – they know how to polish your story so it better speaks to readers. So, if your book might offend readers or make them uncomfortable, they'll let you know so you can amend it.

Why should you care if you offend or trigger readers? Well, if you don't, you may want to google empathy. But in general, your readers are the people who support you, talk about your book, and hopefully make you money. If you're not on their side, why should they invest in you? A book that includes even an accidental micro-aggression can lead to readers losing trust in the author. This can mean an entire author career flushed right down the toilet.

Especially for older generations who aren't so up to date on what's considered appropriate and what isn't today, it can be really tough to conceptualise representation in writing and how to do it well. It can be difficult to understand those who are different to ourselves. There are so many things we say in our language that we may not realise have a negative impact. That's okay. We aren't all born knowing exactly how to say everything right all the time, especially as language is ever evolving, but we can put in the effort to treat each other with as much kindness as we can.

Researching diversity

Language and understanding of culture evolves constant-ly, and if I give certain advice in this book, the correct language could change at any time and this book could therefore misinform people. That's why rather than provide specific advice, I suggest you continue to research and learn, and do the best by your diverse characters and readers.

All writers have to do some level of research to make their story realistic. For example, if I were to write a book about an astronaut, I'd look deeply into what astronauts do, and even try to interview one so I can make sure I got their perspective right. If we're writing about a character who has an experience different to ours, it's up to us to write that experience with authenticity. Of course, when it comes to writing about people from diverse backgrounds and/or minority groups, especially those who are negatively impacted by poor representation and stereotypes, we have a responsibility to do right by them.

There are countless resources out there to help you learn how to write about different communities with authenticity and respect. You might find people on social media who talk about their community, and really listen to what they have to say. You can look at different websites about writing diverse characters, like *Writing with Color*. In general, just listen to the people around you. If you're not sure about something, always ask someone from the actual community you're writing about – they are the expert. That said, don't show up with entitlement and expect people to educate you for free.

Also, remember that diversity isn't necessary in every book. Forcing diversity by lazily including stereotyped characters that lack depth can be worse than simply not including them. Although diversity in characters is amazing, it should be done with genuine care, not as something you feel you should throw in to cover yourself against the 'woke agenda'.

Sensitivity readers

Sensitivity readers play an important role in ensuring your writing accurately represents perspectives and cultures outside of your own experiences. They provide insights and feedback on sensitive topics such as race, ethnicity, gender, sexuality, disability, mental health, and more. I can't recommend them enough for when you're writing on a sensitive topic. These readers bring first-hand experience (and often have also studied and researched the topics they're reading for) to assess how well you portray characters from different communities. Their feedback helps you avoid stereotypes, clichés, and misrepresentations, creating authenticity and promoting inclusivity in your writing.

It isn't just about 'not getting cancelled'. It's about doing your job as an author to ensure that readers don't feel marginalised by books they're supposed to enjoy. Sensitivity reader feedback ensures your writing is respectful, accurate, and considerate to all readers, irrespective of their backgrounds. Incorporating feedback from sensitivity readers widens your understanding of diverse perspectives and helps you grow as a writer. It allows you to approach storytelling with empathy, authenticity, and a more nuanced understanding of the experiences of others.

Some sensitivity readers will be friends who are doing you a favour, or people who are already part of your beta team. They don't have to be professionals – they just have to identify as a member of the minority community you've included in your novel. However, many sensitivity readers are professionals, and they charge a fee for their services. Since sensitivity reading can bring up traumas and triggers, I believe it's important to respect the fees of those who ask for payment. They're offering you an invaluable service, after all.

Resources

Thank you, beautiful writer, for reading this book! I'm so excited for your future, and I hope you got lots out of reading all my advice. If you want to keep hearing from me, you'll most often find me on TikTok and Instagram, at **@poppysvintagebooks**.

I, of course, also offer editing services, so for more personalised feedback and guidance on editing your work, please visit my website **poppyspagesediting.com** to discover how we can work together. Now, onto the resources I promised you!

Firstly, please visit **poppyspagesediting.com/post/fiction-outlining-template** to find my outlining template and sample outline.

Style Sheet

Punctuation

Oxford commas for lists

No semi colons following headings

Single quote marks

En dashes, spaced either side

Numeral ages (30-year-old)

Ellipses spaced out . . .

In-text lists lower case with closed parenthesis, e.g. a), b)

Compound Words

In general, fewer hyphens – prefer putting words together or with a space.

bestsellers/bestselling

en dash/em dash

full time

follow up

in-between

in-depth

likeminded

long haul

metadata

nitty gritty

self publishing

self editing, self publishing, **but** self-doubt, self-esteem

spellcheck

wishlist

word count

worldbuilding

Note: Hyphenate terms like side-by-side, day-to-day, step-by-step

Referencing

Book titles in italics, with the author and year included in-line or in brackets following the title.

Common errors to check/other words

Check that whenever an abbreviation is used for the first time, it's spelled out, then abbreviated all times after.

info dumping becomes exposition dumping (more relevant term)

Check affect and effect

Spell out 'versus' (not vs)

Examples

Example text in italics when it's a full sentence, but in quote marks when it's only a word or two.

Emphasis

Style phrases or words for emphasis with *italics.*

Capitals

Capital letter after colon only if full sentence.

Comments and Track Changes (when referring specifically to Word functions).

For initialisms and acronyms, letters only, no full stops: AKA, ASAP

A plot, B plot

Functions, like Find and Replace or Text-to-Speech

Titles

Title case for Heading 1s (chapter headings) but sentence case for all lower-level headings.

Chapter One

Exceptions

Break the quotes/italics rule ONLY in Style Sheet section where ALL example words or phrases are italics.

Formatting

Paragraphs spaced not indented.

Book graphic to go at end of chapters (before exercise if there is one), but omitted if no room at the bottom of the page.

Round bullet points

Spelling

In general, UK/Australian conventions, like *colour* and *analyse*.

A

acknowledgements

alright

B

big 5 publishers

C

cafe (no accent)

cliché (accented)

E

eBook

ePub

etc. (preferred over etcetera)

G

google (verb) Google (noun)

N

naïve (accented)

P

pt (preferred over 'point' in font sizing)

S

sci-fi, sci-fi and fantasy, SFF

U

UK English, US English (not British English/American English)

Poppy's Pages Worksheets

Character Building Worksheet

As the emotional core of the story, your characters are the most important aspect of novel writing to nail. We're all human (right?) so it makes sense that the humans in a book are what we relate to and therefore emotionally connect to most. This means that our books need strong characters to connect with and root for – otherwise, even if the rest of the story is brilliant, readers will struggle to engage.

Fill out this checklist to take your character from a simple idea or stereotype, to a 'real' person your readers will love.

Character's Name:

Physical

- **Body**
  - Height:
  - Weight:
  - Build:
- **Hair**
  - Texture:
  - Colour:
  - Length:
  - Style:
- **Eyes**
  - Shape:
  - Colour:
  - Eyebrows:
  - Lashes:
- **Skin**
  - Tone:
  - Blemishes:
  - Scars:
- **Face Shape:**
  - Mouth/Lips:
  - Teeth:
  - Chin/Jaw:
  - Nose:

Style:

Grooming:

Accessories:

Mannerisms

How do they walk?

How can you tell they're lying?

What gestures do they tend to use?

What expressions do they often make?

How can you tell when they're upset?

How do they talk?

What's their posture like?

What's their accent?

Do they have any strange quirks?

Personality

Protagonist, Antagonist, or other?

Confident or Nervous?

Academic or Street Smart?

Emotionally Intelligent or Self-Centred?

Relatable or Different?

Optimistic or Pessimistic?

Introvert or Extrovert?

Creative or Unimaginative?

Resourceful or Useless?

Friendly or Hostile?

Defensive or Vulnerable?

Leader or Follower?

Emotional or Logical?

Straightforward or Manipulative?

Honest or Liar?

How do they reach conclusions?

How do they feel emotions?

Myers-Briggs Type:

Zodiac Sign:

Enneagram:

Type A or Type B:

Positives

What drives the character?

What is their motivation?

What are their interests and hobbies?

Are they religious/spiritual?

Who is their favourite character?

What are their special abilities or skills?

What is their dream lifestyle?

What would be their perfect day?

What are their strengths?

What is their most treasured possession?

What length would they go to, to protect this possession?

Who is their hero?

Negatives

Who is their least favourite character?

What types of art do they hate?

What do they regret?

What is their worst memory?

What are their secrets?

What is their tipping point?

What are their weaknesses?

What angers them?

Do they have any bad habits?

The Character's Story

Plot Arc
Why are they in this story? What purpose do they serve?

Do they influence the plot, and does the plot influence them? How?

Development

How do they change throughout the story?

- **Priorities:**

- **Views/Opinions:**

- **Looks:**

- **Knowledge:**

- **Personality:**

- **Relationships:**

Background

Race and Nationality:

Gender and Pronouns:

Birthday and Age:

Decade they grew up in:

Occupation and income:

Class:

Go into more detail

Key Points from Childhood:

Family:

Friends:

Their best experiences:

Their worst experiences:

Worldbuilding Worksheet

Just as we move through physical spaces every day and are affected by the world around us, fictional settings should be detailed enough that the reader feels immersed in them and can see how the characters are affected by the state of the world. This is a vital part of realism in storytelling, and by answering the questions in this worksheet, you'll be able to make your story far more engaging.

Geography

- What does it look like, and what is the overarching aesthetic/feel?

- What's the terrain like?

- What are some important locations?

- What's the weather like?

- Is the world habitable?

- What animals or other creatures live there?

- What are the plants like?

- What are the area's dangers?

- What's the architecture like?

- What building materials do they have/use?

Society

- People
    - What do the people look like?

    - What do they dress like?

    - What are their customs?

    - Are they educated? To what level?

    - What's a day in the life of a citizen?

- Culture
  - What's the history?

  - Do they use any slang?

  - Are they religious? What are their beliefs and religious cultures?

  - What language do they speak?

  - Do they have any traditions?

  - What's the art and music like?

- Government
  - Who's in charge?

  - How does the government/leadership operate?

- Is there money, or trade? Does this economy function well or poorly?

- Do citizens have access to basic human needs?

- Are there ongoing issues or wars?

- Are there any unusual laws? How do law enforcers impose them?

- Life
  - How do people travel?

  - How do people communicate?

  - What are typical family structures and expectations?

  - What are typical work structures and expectations?

  - What are the social/class structures? Is discrimination present?

o What's the level of technology/how is it used?

o What do people eat?

Technology, magic, or other fantastical elements

- How does it affect society?

- How does it affect the world itself?

- What are its parameters and rules?

- What are its benefits?

- What are its dangers?

- Does everyone have access, or only a select few? How do people gain access?

Story

- How does the world affect the story, and vice versa?

- Where does the main character fit into this world?

- How do they navigate the world?

- How does the reader learn about the world?

Plot & Chapter Planning

Stories need structure to make sense and build tension, keeping the reader absorbed and excited throughout. Make sure your book follows some basic 'rules', like those outlined in this worksheet, to give it a boost in engagement!

The Basics

Intended word count:

- Where and when is your story set?

- What genre are you writing, and how will you meet genre expectations or twist them?

- Who's your main character, and what's their journey?

- What's the source of conflict?

- How does the story unfold? What's your overall concept for the beginning, middle, and end?

The Specifics

How do the time, place, and society impact the plot?

Is the story more plot driven or character driven? How do these plot journeys develop?

How does the main character's development affect the plot, and vice versa?

Who are the major characters? Why are they important and how do they develop?

What are the major character arcs and how do the characters develop?

What are the stakes? What's the worst that could happen if the main character doesn't 'win'?

Beginning

The first section of a novel is all about hooking readers by strategically introducing your characters and conflict. This is where a reader will decide if they'll continue or not — if they aren't intrigued now, you might lose them.

When planning the Beginning, consider how you'll give readers the information they need to understand the story. Will you use flashbacks to explain any relevant backstory? Or will you weave the information in, slowly revealing details through conversation and conflict?

The Beginning must simultaneously build mystery and answer questions. Start the first page with action — not an exposition dump. This scene must show readers the stakes of the story and who the main character is. The reader should immediately care, and we do this by giving them an emotional connection to the main character and basic context of the setting.

Word count of section (typically 10-25% of the book):

Characters in this section:

Major events in this section/basic outline:

Character development (where do the characters start, and how do they evolve here?):

Opening scene outline:

Middle

By the Middle of your story, your main character's real life will have been irreversibly shaken up, launching the story into the meat of the plot. Now, they'll begin chasing after their desires, and new information or plot twists will occur to progress the story.

How will you make this section — the largest chunk of your story — lead to the End? What's the journey that your characters embark on? It could be as intense as an epic fantasy expedition to complete a quest, or as simple as a student getting through the school year while juggling the problems of real life. Whatever it is, the journey must be engaging and purposeful, and include several minor conflicts to keep the reader engaged.

Word count of section (typically 50-70% of the book):

Characters in this section:

Major events in this section/basic outline:

Character development:

How this section leads into the End:

End

Now you've arrived at the end of your novel, ready for the big, final conflict and its subsequent resolution. Does your main character win the battle? Do they find happiness? Or is it a tragic ending, in which they lose everything?

It's usually best to have a wrapped-up, satisfying end for your characters. The reader will want to feel good after reading your book, and not like they've missed out on something, or read an entire novel just for the conflict to remain unsolved. (Though you can leave some loose ends if you plan to write a series.)

You'll also need to consider if an epilogue is needed. Many authors add this final bonus chapter at the end to show their characters after the conflict is resolved — how are they dealing with their changed lives?

Word count of section (typically 10-25% of the book):

Characters in this section:

Major events in this section/basic outline:

Character development:

End scene outline:

Sub-Plots

Within your major story arc, which carries the beginning, middle, and end, there'll be interlinked sub-plots that help the characters grow and reach their final destination. These build throughout the story, keeping your audience engaged.

Your sub-plots could be romances, underlying mysteries that need solving, or side quests to complete. They're the smaller goals the characters want to reach, or issues that come up along the way. Sub-plots are great for keeping your readers guessing through the middle section of your book, as they'll create the necessary tension-rise of conflicts and climaxes that lead to the finale.

Answer the following for each subplot:

What's the concept?

What's the purpose? How does it impact the main plot?

Who's involved? Who does it impact, and how/why?

Does it end well, or poorly?

The Chapters

Complete this checklist for each chapter.

Physical — When, Where, and How it Feels

- Time:

- Place:

- Weather/Temperature:

- **The 5 senses:**

    o Sight:

    o Touch:

    o Taste:

    o Smell:

    o Sound:

Story/Plot — What happens?

Purpose (how does the chapter progress the overall arc):

Basic outline:

Important dialogue/action:

Sub-plots:

Characters

Narrator (whose head the reader is in):

How does this chapter progress the main characters through their

development?

What does this chapter reveal about the characters?

What's their mood/emotional journey in this chapter?

Writing

Tone/Emotional Feel of Chapter:

First sentence (to draw in reader):

Last sentence (to make them read the next chapter):

Quotes/ideas for lines:

Self-Editing Checklist

Developmental

- Plot
  - Is there a clear beginning, middle, and end, with subplots and satisfying arcs?
  - Can you identify any plot holes, or events that happen too easily?
  - Does the plot flow naturally, or does it feel forced?
  - Is the pacing effective? Does it feel too rushed or too slow at any point?
  - Are the stakes obvious? Will the reader care and be emotionally connected?
  - Does the conflict seem realistic?
  - Do the plot twists make sense, with necessary foreshadowing?

- Characters
  - Do the characters feel real and well-developed?
  - Are their actions realistic and characteristic?
  - Do they develop throughout the plot?
  - Are they likeable, interesting, or engaging enough to make readers care?
  - Will readers love and hate the right characters?
  - Are their names easy to pronounce/read, and have you avoided similar names?

- Sub-plots
  - Do the sub-plots weave well into the main plot, or feel tacked on?

- o Do they add to the character development and raise the tension?
  - o How do they mirror and influence other arcs in the story?
  - o Are they all tied up by the end?
- World/Setting
  - o Is the world revealed strategically, rather than in exposition dumps?
  - o Is there anything about the world that may confuse readers?
  - o Have you described the senses vividly, so settings will feel real to readers?
  - o Is the time period and place in the world clear?
- Chapters
  - o Do the chapter breaks make sense?
  - o Does each chapter start with a hook?
  - o Does each chapter end with a hook?
- First pages
  - o Does the hook engage the reader immediately?
  - o Does it start with action, not exposition? Does it introduce the characters well, creating an immediate emotional connection?

Copy/Line

- Tone and style
  - o Read the work aloud
  - o Check for showing/telling
  - o Remove redundant words
  - o Rework passive voice
  - o Rework run-on sentences and comma splices

- Remove unnecessary dialogue tags
- Remove adverbs and replace with stronger verbs
- Reduce over-description
- Check that dialogue reads well and doesn't sound awkward
- Check interior monologue. Does it make sense? Is there too much/is it too obvious? Can you cut down long passages?
- Do you overuse any words/phrases?
- Do you overuse any punctuation?
- Have you used clichés?
- Does each character have a unique voice?
- Do you stick to one tense (past/present)?
- Point of View
  - Is the POV clear?
  - Have you avoided head-hopping?
  - Do you always stay in the right POV type (first/second/third)?

Grammar and Spelling (style guide)

- Use a spell checker to identify typos and awkward phrasing.
- Check that dialogue/quotes are punctuated correctly.
- Check you've used the right spelling for your country (UK vs US English).
- Check your punctuation use is consistent, e.g. em dashes and en dashes.

The Book

- Are the chapter numbers correct?

- Are the page numbers correct?

- Are the font, design, and formatting consistent?

- Are paragraphs indented correctly (0.5in hanging except first lines in sections)?

eBook Publishing

To-Do List

Title

- Catchy title to entice readers
- Name of series in brackets

Blurb

- Suited to your genre
- Starts with a great hook
- Mentions comparative titles and/or quotes from reviews
- Call to action

Keywords

- Anything that relates to your book that isn't in the title or description
- What people may search for
- Genre and comparative titles

Cover

- Professionally designed cover
    - Easy to read
    - Draws the eye

- o Represents your genre
- o Represents the themes of your book

ePub

- Professionally formatted ePub file of the book (to Kindle standards)
- Chapters are easy to navigate
- Book has been copyedited and proofread

Pricing

- Priced competitively
- Choose your royalty rate (research for each publishing platform)
- Price for each country individually to ensure a sellable price

Promotions and Ads

- Allow pre-orders before publication (promote on social media)
- Price promotions (freebies and sales)
- New Release campaigns
- Email Newsletter campaigns
- Amazon Ads

Blurb Writing Guide

What it needs to include

In your blurb, you have up to 300 words to not only describe your book, but SELL it.

- Start with a hook (which can be used across your marketing)
    - A question that asks, What If?
    - A phrase that establishes the stakes
    - A phrase that introduces the main character
- Describe the story — but not too much
    - Why will readers love the characters?
    - Define the stakes (what's the most intense aspect to this story?)
    - Define the tone and genre
    - Use a cliff-hanger effect to entice readers to open the book
- Call to Action — why buy it?
- Quote from book or review as 'evidence'

How to word it

A 'perfect' blurb won't work if it's written in the wrong style. Remember that the blurb isn't used to impress readers — it's to pique their interest and convince them to buy the book. Write it:

- In the same tone as your book, to give readers a feel for your style
- Free of spoilers (not including the inciting incident)
- With Search Engine Optimised keywords
- Using positive language
- In short, easy to consume paragraphs

Search other books in your genre and see how the blurbs are written. Would you deem them successful or unsuccessful? Would those blurbs convince you to read the books? Find the best, and consider how you can apply their methods to your own blurb.

Author Website Checklist

Your Author Website is your space to show potential readers why they should buy your books, tell current readers more about yourself, and reward your most loyal fans. It must encapsulate who you are as an author, be a point for making sales, and lead to your other marketing methods such as mailing list and social media.

Header

- Your Name – Author
- Your logo
- Menu
    - About
    - Books
    - Press/Events
    - News/Blog
    - Contact
- Links to social media
- Link to newsletter signup

Footer

- Contact details
- Logo
- Copyright
- Links to social media

Home Page

- Your latest release and bestseller
- Links to Amazon (or where your books are available)
- Short Bio – linked to About Page
- Contact Form

- Newsletter Signup (with reader magnet)
- 5 Star Reviews (2-4)

About Page

- Expand on your Author Bio
- Why do you write your books, and what gives you the authority to write them?
- Give insight into your life – Where do you write? Do you have another job? What are your hobbies?
- A professional photo of yourself

Books Page

- Include all of your books, with links to separate pages for each book with more information
- Book covers, titles, years, and hook
- **Individual pages**: pages for each book should look similar to how they look on Amazon (copy your blurb), but here you have more creative freedom. Make sure to include the link so people can buy it, as well as a call to action.

Press/Events

Even if you don't have significant press/events, include this page (with at least some posts) to increase your credibility as a 'real author'.

- Add news and press releases that don't fit on your blog
- Add your media kit
- Add a contact form for press to contact you
    - Mention that you're always happy to have your book reviewed (so bloggers/reviewers also know they can contact you)
    - If you have a separate publicist or assistant who handles enquiries, make sure to add their details

Blog

Your blog can be anything you want it to be, but in general it's a place to give your readers an insight into your life and a behind-the-scenes look at the books they love to read.

- Your writing process
- Updates on your writing
- Reviews of books you're reading
- Announcing new releases
- Announcing promotions and sales

Contact

Your super-fan readers may want a way to contact you to talk about your book, so it's a good idea to have a clear contact form for them.

- You can simply copy + paste the contact widget you used in your homepage or press page
- Consider privacy when deciding whether or not to add your phone number/address

The Branding

The look of your site should follow the genre you write in and tone of your books. A romance site will be dark and romantic, while a children's site will be busy and colourful.

- Which fonts will you use? Are they clear and branded?
  - Avoid using fancy fonts — many authors make this mistake as they want their website to suit their genre and look interesting, but it makes the content much harder to consume for the reader
- Add images that represent your book and draw the eye

The Wording

The way you write on your website can be a first impression for readers as to whether they like your style or not.

- Write in the same tone as your book to give readers a feel for your style
- Make sure to not include major spoilers
- Using SEO keywords
  - Make use of headings and sub-headings
- Keep text short and sweet, separated into small paragraphs to retain attention (Remember, this is a digital platform, not a novel!)
- Use a spellchecker like Grammarly to check for errors

Social Media Marketing Starter Guide

As an author, your social media platforms are a vital marketing tool in reaching potential readers and retaining fans. With options for both organic and paid reach, you can get sales through SMM even with a small budget.

Before you create accounts

- *Research your book's audience*
    - *Which platforms are they using?*
    - *What are other successful authors with your genre/audience doing?*
    - *How are users and creators using these platforms?*
- *Pick 2-3 traditional platforms (don't try to do all of them unless you have time)*

Major platforms include:

Facebook:

- Create a business page, and even a group, to connect with readers and writers
- Facebook is notorious for poor engagement for business pages — rather than focus on this, work on deepening relationships with top fans here

Instagram:

- Focus on visuals. What do your readers want to see?
- Build your community by interacting as much as you can. Like, comment, share, and save posts from authors and readers
- Use popular hashtags like #bookstagram #amwriting #writersofinstagram

LinkedIn:

- LinkedIn is a great place to be seen as a professional writer and connect with others in the publishing industry
- Post frequently and engage with other people to expand your network — you never know who you might find here

Twitter/X:

- The home of short and simple posting, Twitter is great for getting out quick messages
- The #writercommunity is a great place to connect with other authors and grow your following
- Threads is Instagram's version of Twitter, which is also a great place to grow your community and build on your Instagram

Pinterest:

- Create your own posts, or 'pin' other posts to your 'boards'
- Create boards with inspiration for your books (book aesthetic boards)
- Direct readers, from your other socials, to visit your boards and see the visual aspect of your book (inspiration, style/aesthetic, etc.)
- Post quotes and images that reflect your books and lead to your website

TikTok:

- This short video platform has amazing community called 'Booktok', that has done a lot to boost the publishing industry since 2020
- Create videos of varying lengths and following different trends to see what your audience responds well to
- Tell stories in video form, or use viral 'sounds' and apply them to your situation
- Don't worry about being polished here — people find casual creators more relatable

Running Ads & Campaigns

Ads are vital to many authors, especially those self publishing, because the ads target the specific audience directly.

1. Decide on your audience, and be as specific as possible (try several to find what works)

2. Decide what you're selling — is this ad about sales, engagement, newsletter signups, etc.?

3. Choose your visual — a photo of your book, a graphic, a quote, or other related image

4. Write the copy — include an engaging caption and a call to action that encourages clicks

5. Consider your bid — when starting with ads, keep your budget low to test (increase gradually)

6. Evaluate ads over time to see what's working

Posts

The great thing about social media marketing is its organic (unpaid) reach. This is a place to build community with readers all over the world. Building a following — before your book is even published — is a fantastic way to create momentum and connect with fans. Just like in your ads, use engaging images and copy, but you can be more 'real' in your day-to-day posts. This is where you talk to readers as if they're your friends, and avoid obvious selling.

Writing Updates

- Behind-the-scenes (writing space, inspiration, meetings)
- Teasers & samples
- Events
- Release dates

User-Generated Content

- Reviews of your book
- Photos of your book, fanart, and cosplays

Challenges and Giveaways

- Create competitions for readers to win your books or merchandise
- Create rules such as having to share your post, follow you, and comment + tag a friend to increase engagement

Other

- Polls
- Interaction in groups
- Interaction in hashtags
- Livestreams

Branding

- Your social media pages should look and feel like you, matching your branding that you use across your books, website, and more
- Always use the same filter or editing presets on images so they look cohesive
- Stick to the same fonts, font colours, and emojis
- Cultivate a 'voice' that feels like you but is more strategic in terms of engaging readers and selling books

Do you want to read my novels?

The WOKEN KINGDOM series is available anywhere you buy books online. Here's the blurb for book one:

*

A hundred years ago, a dark fairy cursed an innocent princess, forcing a kingdom to sleep until a brave prince would save them.

Maya is fueled by spite towards the royal family and fairies, who trapped ordinary people like her in a curse they didn't deserve. Now poverty-stricken, the seventeen-year-old bookmaker has one goal: rob her grandmother's faraway grave and use the riches within to save her family from starvation.

As she enters a world she doesn't recognise, Maya meets the charismatic but mysterious Teddy. He agrees to help her, and it's only a matter of time before romantic feelings emerge. But when Teddy's secret is revealed, it doesn't only change their friendship - it changes Maya's entire world.

To reach the enchanted treasure she seeks, Maya will need blessings from each of the seven fairies. She and Teddy journey across each of the fairies' distinct territories, experiencing mystical powers, stunning cities, and lush landscapes. Even with a deadly rival close behind, Maya won't be stopped. But she is yet to learn the true cost of her treasure.

When Maya must choose between saving her family or stopping a lurking evil, who will she betray?

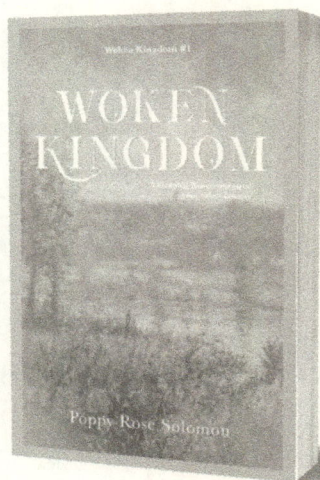

www.ingramcontent.com/pod-product-compliance
Lightning Source LLC
Chambersburg PA
CBHW022129020426
42334CB00015B/825